Sweet Medicine

Sweet Medicine

Sites of Indian Massacres, Battlefields, and Treaties

Photographs by Drex Brooks

Essay by Patricia Nelson Limerick
Foreword by James Welch

UNIVERSITY OF NEW MEXICO PRESS
Albuquerque

Grateful acknowledgment is made to the following publishers for permission to reprint this material:

Excerpts from *Black Elk Speaks,* by John G. Neihardt. Copyright © 1961 by the University of Nebraska Press. Reprinted by permission.

From *Life of George Bent,* by George E. Hyde. Copyright © 1968 by the University of Oklahoma Press. Reprinted by permission.

From *A History of the Indians of the United States,* by Angie Debo. Copyright © 1970 by the University of Oklahoma Press. Reprinted by permission.

From *The Way to Rainy Mountain,* by N. Scott Momaday. Copyright © 1969 by the University of New Mexico Press. Reprinted by permission.

From *The Indian and the White Man,* by Chandler Whipple. Copyright © 1976 by the Berkshire Traveller Press. Reprinted by permission.

Library of Congress Cataloging-in-Publication Data

Brooks, Drex, 1952–
    Sweet medicine: sites of Indian massacres, battlefields, and treaties / photographs by Drex Brooks ; essay by Patricia Nelson Limerick ; foreword by James Welch. — 1st ed.
      p.   cm.
    Includes bibliographical references.
    ISBN 0-8263-1538-0.
    1. Indians of North America—Wars.   2. Battlefields—United States—Pictorial works.   3. Indians of North America—History—Pictorial works.   4. United States—History—Pictorial works.   I. Limerick, Patricia Nelson, 1951– . II. Title.
E81.B7   1995
973—dc20   94-6689
                                  CIP

Printed in Canada.

Contents

Acknowledgments
ix

Foreword
James Welch
xi

Plates
1

Haunted America
Patricia Nelson Limerick
119

Notes
161

For Fanny Chargingshield, Cooking Look, Dora Morning, and all the others.

Acknowledgments

Many people helped make this book possible including those who put me up in their homes while I was traveling and photographing, and those who directed me to sites. I especially wish to thank the man who owned the land on which the Sand Creek Massacre site is located (he drove me around the site one afternoon) and the woman in Greenville, Ohio, who went out of her way to lead me through traffic to the Greenville Treaty site. There were many other similar acts of kindness, too numerous to mention here.

I would like to thank the Native Americans in general and Rayna Green and Edgar Heap-of-Birds in particular for their words of encouragement in the early phases of this project. A portion of any profits I receive from sales of this book will be made available to the American Indian College Fund.

The people at UNM Press, Ruth Thorne-Thomsen and Ray Metzker, Stephen Brigidi, Stephen Petegorsky, Hallie Joyce, and Mark Biddle have my appreciation for their help with editing and design. Thanks to my teachers and to the Williams family for their support over the years. And thanks to Amy Adams for everything.

This book would not have been possible without the financial assistance I received from the National Endowment for the Arts, The Ludwig Vogelstein Foundation, Art Matters Incorporated, the Utah Arts Council, and Weber State University. I am especially grateful to the Department of Visual Arts at Weber State University for time off to photograph and for the office help and friendship provided by Elaine Luhn and Laura McBeth.

Foreword

"News came to us there in the moon of the Falling Leaves that the Black Hills had been sold to the Wasichus and also all the country west of the Hills— the country we were in then. I learned when I was older that our people did not want to do this. The Wasichus went to some of the chiefs and got them to put their marks on the treaty. Maybe some of them did this when they were crazy from drinking the minne wakan the Wasichus gave them. I have heard this; I do not know. But only crazy or very foolish men would sell their Mother Earth. Sometimes I think it might have been better if we had stayed together and made them kill us all."

Black Elk, a Lakota, was speaking of the loss of the Black Hills, but he might have been speaking of the losses suffered by all Indians in this country. Sacred places, hunting grounds, territory—or just favorite spots to pick chokecherries, to court a lover, or to find the right wood to make arrows and bowls— all were taken from the first people by the invasion of the Wasichus, the whites.

In 1992, we celebrated in this country the quincentenary of the arrival of that quintessential invader, Christopher Columbus. Never mind the fact that the Vikings had already built settlements in North America many hundreds of years before Columbus, we have chosen to celebrate the Italian explorer as the discoverer of America. What did he bring to the New World? Civilization, Christianity, cruelty, ethnocentrism, and disease. Fortunately, neither he nor those who followed him were absolutely successful in replacing the civilizations of the natives, but it wasn't for want of trying. Consequently, the United States is littered with battle sites, treaty sites, and areas of great beauty and of great potential that have been forcibly taken from the Indians.

Drex Brooks, a remarkable picture-taker, has provided us with photographs that document these sites, many of which have become sacred through tragedy. The social commentary in these landscape portraits, as well as the written comments that accompany many of them, is both understated and overwhelming. Several of these sites are lonely, as is much of the wide open western space, giving one the feeling that the significance has faded from the national consciousness. Other sites are close by but equally forgotten, in the middle of a Nebraska cornfield or along a seldom traveled highway in Tennessee. Of course, many are national historical sites, but even these tend to provide the tourist only a momentary view of a distant event. Drex Brooks captures with his camera the paradox that history, for many of us, is a series of undistinguished tributaries that make up the great stream of the United States of America.

How does he do this? By rejecting the idea that each event should trickle into the whole. These photographs are about particularity, from Plymouth Rock to the Fallen Timbers Battlefield in Ohio, from the LaPointe Treaty Site in Wisconsin to the Crazy Woman Battlefield in Wyoming. The clarity of the images removes any doubt that things important happened in these corners of America. Whether it be an Indian cemetery at Carlisle or a vast snow field in California, we are forced by the power of the photographs into a feeling of participation. Each one of us, Indian and white, is a part of this history.

As a Blackfeet Indian, I was especially moved by a scene that is close to me—the Marias River Massacre site. Here, during a smallpox winter, 173 people of the peace chief Heavy Runner's band, mostly women, children, and old ones (as the men were off hunting) were murdered by the United States Army. My great-grandmother was wounded but managed to escape, along with some other women and children. Now the site is forgotten, not even a marker to commemorate the Blackfeet dead.

These are not romantic pictures—the dead raccoon in the snowy field, the stark white tombstones at the cemetery, the Trailways tour bus at the Sand Creek Massacre site, the child at Plymouth Rock— the slightly off-center but always right-on nature of the photographs tells us that lives end but history pushes on.

This frank quality extends to the sometimes moving, sometimes straightforward, sometimes ironic captions. For instance, the text that accompanies the Plymouth Rock picture is a marvel of dark humor: "The Pilgrim Fathers landed on the shores of America and fell upon their knees. Then they fell upon the aborigines. (Author Unknown)." Other texts are more conventional, many of them speeches by important chiefs, writings by army officers, words on highway markers, remarks made by simple-minded bureaucrats ("Kill the Indian and save the man!"). All the texts are wonderfully appropriate—for better or worse.

This book will move you because it is a pictorial chronicle of the many battles, massacres, and broken treaties that led directly to the dire Indian condition today. Drex Brooks pulls no punches. His is a brave, true look at a shameful, neglected moment in the history of mankind. For that, we all must thank him.

James Welch

Plates

The greatest assembly ever of the tribes of the northern plains was held on the North Platte River at the mouth of Horse Creek in September of 1851. Over 10,000 people from the Lakota, Cheyenne, Arapahoe, Crow, Shoshoni, Assiniboine, Blackfeet, and other tribes met to make a mutual and lasting peace among the tribes and with the U.S. Government. This treaty was meant by the U.S. to define tribal landholdings and boundaries, to put an end to intertribal warfare, and to provide safe passage for the whites traveling the Oregon Trail. But the Mormon Cow Incident, which led to the Grattan Massacre in 1854 and the subsequent massacre of the Brule Lakotas at Ash Hollow in 1855, made the treaty meaningless and set the stage for warfare in the northern plains for the next thirty-five years.

At last Sweet Medicine said to the people: "I shall not be with you long now, I am getting to be old, and have lived as long as I want to; but before I die I have something to tell you. He pointed to the south, and said: Far away in that direction is another kind of buffalo, with long hair hanging down its neck and a tail that drags on the ground. This animal you shall ride on. The buffalo will disappear; and when the buffalo are gone the next animal you will have to eat will be spotted. Soon you will find among you a people who have hair all over their faces, and whose skin is white. They will be looking for a certain stone; they will be people who do not get tired, but will keep pushing forward, going all the time. They will keep coming, coming. They will travel everywhere, looking for this stone which our great-grandfather put on the earth in many places. These people will not listen to what you say; what they are going to do they will do. You people will change; in the end of your life in those days you will not get up early in the morning, you will not know when day comes. They will try to change you from your way of living to theirs. They will tear up the earth, and at last you will do it with them. When you do, you will become crazy, and will forget all that I am teaching you. The white people will be all over the land, and at last you will disappear. I am sorry to say these things, but I have seen them, and you will find that they come true."

—The Prophecy of Sweet Medicine to the Cheyenne People

COUNCIL GROUNDS AT THE GREAT TREATY OF HORSE CREEK, SCOTTS BLUFF COUNTY, NEBRASKA, 1987

The site of the landing of the *Mayflower* in 1620. The local Indians, led by Massasoit, helped the colony survive its first winter. Massasoit's statue stands on the hill overlooking Plymouth Rock.

The Pilgrim fathers landed on the shores of America and fell upon their knees. Then they fell upon the aborigines.

—Author unknown

PLYMOUTH ROCK, PLYMOUTH, MASSACHUSETTS, 1991

Erected A.D. 1889, By the State of Connecticut, To Commemorate the Heroic Achievement of Major John Mason and His Comrades Who Near This Spot, in 1637, Overthrew the Pequot Indians, and Preserved the Settlements From Destruction.

—Inscription on the base of the statue of John Mason in Mystic, Connecticut

All in all, seventy wigwams and their contents were destroyed, women and children burned alive and those braves who tried to tomahawk their assailants were slain with the sword. Only seven captives were taken, and about that number escaped. At least four or five hundred of the Pequots were killed, and some estimates place the figure as high as six hundred. Two of the English were killed, and around twenty wounded.

As Captain Underhill later wrote:
   Many courageous fellows fought most desperately through the palisades so that they scorched and burned with the very flame . . . and so perished valiantly. Mercy did they deserve for their valor, could we have had the opportunity to bestow it. Many were burned in the fort, both men, women and children. Others, forced out, came in troops . . . twenty and thirty at a time, which our soldiers received and entertained with the point of a sword. . . . Great and doleful was the bloody sight, to the view of young soldiers who had never been in war to see so many souls lie gasping on the ground so thick in some places that you could hardly pass along. It was a fearful sight to see them frying in the fire and the streams of blood quenching the same and horrible was the stink and stench thereof. But the victory seemed a sweet sacrifice and they gave praise thereof to God.

Paraphrased from *The Indian and the White Man in New England* by Chandler Whipple (Stockbridge, Ma.: Berkshire Traveller Press, 1976), pp. 231–32.

MYSTIC MASSACRE SITE, MYSTIC, CONNECTICUT, 1991

Anawan Rock-Squanakonk Swamp, Site of the Capture of Chief Anawan, Wampanoag Indian, by Benjamin Church in August 1676, Ending King Philip's War.

—Massachusetts Historical Marker at the site

I have thought fit to publish the same; and I do hereby promise, That there shall be paid out of the Province Treasury to all and any of the said forces, over and above their Bounty upon Enlistment, their Wages and Subsistence, Premiums of Bounties following, viz.

For every Male Indian Prisoner above the age of Twelve Years, that shall be taken and brought to *Boston, Fifty Pounds.*

For every Male Indian Scalp, brought in as evidence of their being killed, *Forty Pounds.*

For every Female Indian Prisoner, taken and brought in as aforesaid, and for every Male Indian Prisoner under the age of Twelve Years, taken and brought in as aforesaid, *Twenty-five Pounds.*

For every Scalp of such Female Indian or Male Indian under Twelve Years of Age, brought as Evidence of their being killed, as aforesaid, *Twenty Pounds.*

Given under my Hand at *Boston,* in the Province aforesaid, this Twelfth Day of June, 1755 (*etc.*)
By His Excellency's Command
J. Willard, Secr'y

W. Shirley

GOD SAVE THE KING

From a facsimile reproduction of the Pioneer Historical Society, cited in *This Country Was Ours: A Documentary History of the American Indian* by Virgil J. Vogel (New York: Harper Torchbooks, 1974), p. 52.

Site of the Capture of Chief Anawan at Anawan Rock in Squanakonk Swamp, Bristol County, Massachusetts, 1991

Metacom, known to the colonists as King Philip, was the leader of the Indians in King Philip's War in their attempt to drive the colonists out of New England. After his death in 1676 his body was quartered and hung in trees. His head was sent to Plymouth and stuck on a pole where it remained for nearly a quarter of a century. Metacom was the son of Massasoit, without whose help the Plymouth colony would not have survived its first year.

SITE OF THE KILLING OF METACOM (KING PHILIP), BRISTOL COUNTY, RHODE ISLAND, 1991

On March 8, 1782, ninety-six Moravian Christian Delaware Indians living at the Gnadenhutten Mission were massacred by American settlers under the command of Colonel David Williams. These defenseless and peaceful Indians were killed in retaliation for raids and killings committed mostly by the Shawnees and Wyandots.

Bishop Loskiel, in his "History of the Missions of the United Brethren," says that the converts were informed that evening of the fate which awaited them, and that they spent the night in praying, singing hymns, and exhorting one another to die with the fortitude of Christians. Men were shaking one another by the hand and kissing one another. Tears were streaming down some faces, while others were full of lines of agony. Agonized mothers, with tears streaming down their swarthy faces, held their children in close embrace.

Accordingly, on the morning of Friday, March 8th, 1782, the terrible decree was carried into execution. The Indian men were led two by two to the cooper shop, where they were beaten to death with mallets and hatchets. The women and children were led into the church and there slaughtered. Many of them died with prayers on their lips, while others met their death chanting songs. Altogether forty men, twenty women, and thirty-four children were inhumanely butchered. Many of the children were brained in their wretched mothers' arms. One of the murderers after having broken the skulls of fourteen of the Christian Delawares, with a cooper's mallet, handed the bloodstained weapon to a companian with the remark: "My arm fails me, go on with the work. I think I have done pretty well." Only two Indians escaped.

From *The Indian Wars of Pennsylvania* by C. Hale Sipe (Harrisburg, Pa.: Telegraph Press, 1929), pp. 649–50.

Gnadenhutten Massacre Site, Gnadenhutten State Monument, Ohio, 1991

On August 20, 1794, General "Mad" Anthony Wayne commanding U.S. troops defeated the Six Nations Confederacy of Indians who had allied themselves with the British, who were trying to maintain economic control of the Old Northwest. After the battle the British, not wanting to risk warfare with the United States, refused the Indians aid and protection after their defeat. The Indian power to resist the invasion of their homelands was broken and the U.S. gained control of the Northwest Territory the following summer at the Treaty of Greenville.

We could not stand against the sharp ends of their guns . . . and we ran to the river, swamps, thickets, and to the islands in the river, covered with corn. Our moccasins trickled blood in the sand, and the water was red in the river. Many of our braves were killed in the river by rifle fire.

—Indian account of the defeat at Fallen Timbers from *President Washington's Indian War* by Wiley Sword (Norman: University of Oklahoma Press, 1985), p. 305.

Fallen Timbers Battlefield, Fallen Timbers State Memorial, Ohio, 1991

Following the crushing defeat of the Six Nations Confederacy at Fallen Timbers, General "Mad" Anthony Wayne concluded an important treaty on August 3, 1795, at Greenville, Ohio, with the following vanquished tribes: Delaware, Wyandot, Shawnee, Ottawa, Chippewa, Potawatomi, Miami, Eel River, Wea, Kickapoo, Piankashaw, and Kaskaskia. The United States gave the Indians rights to occupy the land lying between the Cuyahoga River and the Mississippi, which allowed them to hunt in northern Ohio as well as in the territory now comprising Indiana and Illinois. The government reserved for itself nearly seventeen million acres in eastern and southern Ohio, embracing about two-thirds of the state, from which the Indians had to move. The Greenville Treaty opened up the Northwest Territory, and as the Indians departed, the Americans seized control of the Ohio River Valley.

—Paraphrased from *The Delaware Indians: A History* by C. A. Weslager (New Brunswick, N. J.: Rutgers University Press, 1972), p. 333.

GREENVILLE TREATY SITE, GREENVILLE, OHIO, 1991

Spanish soldiers may have fired from this very site during the infamous "massacre" of 1805. Their Navajo targets were huddled in the alcove below.

Spanish accounts describe an ongoing battle against the Indians—"entrenched in an almost inaccessible point"—and the killing of ninety warriors and twenty-five women and children. The Navajo, however, say many men were away hunting at the time. Thus the dead were mostly women, children, and old men who had sought refuge from the invaders.

The Navajo call the alcove *Adah Aho'doo'nili*—Two Fell Off—referring to a brave Navajo woman who grappled with a soldier and tumbled to her death, dragging the enemy with her.

—On the marker at the site

PLACE WHERE TWO FELL OFF, CANYON DE CHELLEY NATIONAL MONUMENT, ARIZONA, 1990

Holy Ground was one of the main towns of the Creek people, who believed that it was consecrated by being the residence of their principal prophets. They believed that their
enemies could not penetrate its borders and even though the
Creek warriors fanatically defended their sacred town, they
were defeated on December 23, 1813, by troops under the
command of General F. L. Claiborne. Thirty-three Creek
warriors and one American were killed and the town was
looted and burned. The Creeks made their way to join
others of their tribe at Horseshoe Bend where almost 1,000
of their people were killed by U.S. troops under the command of General Andrew Jackson in February of 1814. In
August the Creeks surrendered one-half of present-day Alabama. By the time Alabama became a state in 1819 at least
three-quarters of the state had been ceded by the Indians.
By a series of treaties between 1828 and 1835 there was no
Indian land left in Alabama.

HOLY GROUND BATTLEFIELD, LOWNDES COUNTY, ALABAMA, 1990

Here On September 27, 1830 Was Signed The Treaty Of
Dancing Rabbit Creek. The Choctaw Nation Of Indians Re-
linquished Their Lands To The U.S. And Removed West Of
The Mississippi.

—Inscription on the marker in the Indian graveyard at Dancing
Rabbit Creek Treaty Site.

DANCING RABBIT CREEK TREATY SITE, NOXUBEE COUNTY, MISSISSIPPI, 1990

In April of 1832 Black Hawk and about 1,000 of his Sauk people crossed into Illinois from Iowa Territory to where they had been forcibly removed the year prior. The government sent troops in pursuit, and Black Hawk's War lasted only fifteen weeks, ending August 2, 1832, at the Battle of Bad Axe. By the end of this war approximately two-thirds of Black Hawk's people were dead. After the massacre of the Sauk people at Bad Axe on the Mississippi River, Black Hawk surrendered and was imprisoned at Jefferson Barracks, Missouri.

After holding off his pursuers at the Battle of Wisconsin Heights, Black Hawk led his people over unfamiliar country toward the Mississippi. In the meantime, the army alerted Fort Crawford at Prairie du Chien. When the Indians reached the Mississippi they found an armed steamboat blocking escape. The Battle of Bad Axe fought here August 1–2, 1832 ended the Black Hawk War. Driven into the water by their pursuers, the Indians—warriors, old people, women and children—were shot down or drowned as they tried to escape. Black Hawk succeeded in getting away but was soon taken prisoner. Later when asked about his ill-fated venture he said simply: "Rock River was a beautiful country; I loved my towns, my cornfields, and the home of my people. I fought for it."

—Wisconsin Historical Marker at Bad Axe Massacre Site

Bad Axe Massacre Site, Vernon County, Wisconsin, 1991

At the Cherokee General Council held at Red Clay in October of 1835 the proposed Removal Treaty was rejected by an almost unanimous vote of the approximately 16,000 Cherokee people in attendance there. The treaty was later signed at New Echota, Georgia, by a small minority of Cherokees known as the Treaty Party. This fraudulent treaty was ratified by the U.S. Congress. Under Cherokee law, the members of the Treaty Party sentenced themselves to death by selling Cherokee land, and some of these people were later killed in Oklahoma.

Red Clay Council Grounds, Red Clay State Historical Area, Tennessee, 1991

After rejection of the Removal Treaty by an overwhelming majority of Cherokees at Red Clay in Tennessee, a small group of Cherokees known as the Treaty Party led by Major Ridge and Stand Watie believing removal was inevitable, began negotiating with the federal government. The Senate ratified the fraudulent treaty despite knowledge that only a small minority of Cherokees had accepted it. Over 15,000 Cherokees signed a petition protesting the treaty made at New Echota in December of 1835. By 1838 only 2,000 of the 16,000 Cherokees had removed to Oklahoma, and the government sent in troops to force compliance with the Treaty of New Echota. The Cherokees were rounded up and driven into stockades scattered throughout the Cherokee country. One of these "removal forts" was located at New Echota.

I witnessed the execution of the most brutal order in the history of American warfare. I saw the helpless Cherokees dragged from their homes, and driven at the bayonet point into the stockades. And in the chill of a drizzling rain on an October morning I saw them loaded like cattle or sheep into six hundred and forty-five wagons and headed for the West.

Private John G. Burnett, 1838, from "Trail of Tears National Historic Trail, draft comprehensive management and use plan and environmental assessment," United States Department of the Interior and National Park Service, Denver Service Center (Washington, D.C.: U.S. Government Printing Office, 1991), p. 9.

New Echota, Cherokee Capital and Treaty Site, New Echota State Historical Site, Georgia, 1991

Nearly 10,000 descendants of a small remnant of Cherokees who avoided removal from their homelands in the 1830s live on this reservation in western North Carolina.

EASTERN CHEROKEE RESERVATION, CHEROKEE, NORTH CAROLINA, 1990

In 1837 smallpox first came to the northern plains, carried to the Upper Missouri River by the American Fur Company's steamer *St. Peter*. The disease nearly obliterated the Mandan tribe, then spread to the Arikaras and north and west to the Assiniboine, Gros Ventre, and Blackfeet tribes.

At the mouth of the Little Missouri (a short distance downstream from Fort Union), a Blackfeet Indian was allowed to board the disease-ridden steamer; when he left he became a messenger of death. Although the traders knew they had made a mistake in letting the Indian on board, they did not stop him from leaving.

—Paraphrased from *The Harrowing of Eden: White Attitudes Toward Native Americans* by J. E. Chamberlain (New York: Seabury Press, 1975), p. 105.

Contact and conflict with Europeans had a catastrophic impact on the Indian nations. Contact was by far the greater villain, although conflict has received the publicity. Disease was the sword with which the New World was devastated. European afflictions such as smallpox, tuberculosis, plague, and influenza, unknown to the Americas, found in the aboriginal population highly susceptible victims and proved stunningly efficient killers. Sherburne Cook estimates that in the years 1630 to 1730 diseases introduced by Europeans reduced the native population of New England by approximately 80 percent. In only five years—from 1615 to 1620—between 75 and 90 percent of the Massachusetts tribe died of plague; a decade later more of them succumbed to smallpox.

Of all the diseases introduced by Europeans, smallpox was the most grimly effective. A persuasive argument can be made that smallpox was the single most important factor in the decline of Native American population and power and, therefore, in the success of the European invasion. Successive epidemics swept over the Americas, occasionally yielding fatality rates in single tribes of 90 percent or more. In the late eighteenth and early nineteenth centuries major epidemics, often carried to the Indians by fur traders, crisscrossed the Great Plains, devastating numerous groups. Both the Assiniboines and the Arikaras are believed to have lost half their numbers. The Mandans fared even worse. There were approximately nine thousand of them in 1750. In subsequent decades three waves of the disease struck and virtually annihilated them. By 1837, writes Edward Bruner, "there were only twenty-three male survivors." In some cases disease so reduced native populations that areas that once supported substantial communities were left totally uninhabited and were discovered so by Europeans, whose diseases had silently preceded them. Observes Francis Jennings: "Europeans did not find a wilderness here; rather, however involuntarily, they made one"

From *The Return of the Native: American Indian Political Resurgence* by Stephen Cornell (New York: Oxford University Press, 1988), p. 52.

SMALLPOX INTRODUCTION SITE, FORT UNION TRADING POST, FORT UNION NATIONAL HISTORIC SITE, NORTH DAKOTA, 1989

In August 1854, Commissioner Manypenny directed Agents
Gilbert and Herriman to arrange for the treaty meeting at
La Pointe—the most important event in Chippewa history
since the coming of the white man. The year 1854 was a
turning point for the Lake Superior bands. It climaxed
the traumatic times of the previous forty years and fore-
shadowed even greater cultural changes during the next
century. . . . Prior to 1854 the Chippewas had enjoyed the
freedom of adopting only those features of white culture
which appealed to them. The luxury of selectivity was no
longer theirs; when the chiefs touched their pens to the La
Pointe treaty the bands began a new journey down the white
man's road. For nearly a century it was a road without turning, a one-way street to cultural disintegration and crushing
poverty.

From *The Chippewas of Lake Superior* by Edmund Jefferson Dan-
ziger, Jr., Civilization of the American Indian Series, vol. 148
(Norman: University of Oklahoma Press, 1978), pp. 89–90.

La Pointe Treaty Site, La Pointe, Wisconsin, 1991

This land-cession treaty of 1855 as well as many other treaties are still being contested in court by Native Americans who are being deprived of their treaty rights and lands. The State of Washington has been notorious for its failure to provide fishing rights as outlined in the Point Elliot Treaty and other treaties made by Territorial Governor Stevens during the same time period.

Every part of this soil is sacred, in the estimation of my people. Every hillside, every valley, every plain and grove, has been hallowed by some sad or happy event in days long vanished. Even the rocks, which seem to be dumb and dead as they swelter in the sun along the silent shore thrill with memories of stirring events connected with the lives of my people, and the very dust upon which you now stand responds more lovingly to their footsteps than to yours, because it is rich with the dust of our ancestors and our bare feet are conscious of the sympathetic touch.

And when the last Red Man shall have perished, and the memory of my tribe shall have become a myth among the white man, these shores will swarm with the invisible dead of my tribe, and when your children's children think themselves alone in the field, the store, the shop, upon the highway, or in the silence of the pathless woods, they will not be alone. . . . At night when the streets of your cities and villages are silent and you think them deserted, they will throng with the returning hosts that once filled them and still love this beautiful land. The White Man will never be alone.

Let him be just and deal kindly with my people, for the dead are not powerless. Dead—I say? There is no death. Only a change of worlds.

—Excerpt from a longer speech alleged to have been made by Chief Sealth (Seattle), Duwamish at the signing of the Treaty of Point Elliot on January 22, 1855.

Point Elliot Treaty Site, Mukilteo, Washington, 1991

U.S. troops under Captain Andrew Smith were sent in May of 1856 to meet surrendering Rogue River Indians at Big Meadows on the Rogue River in southwestern Oregon. Parties of Indians coming into surrender were attacked and, in some instances, massacred by white volunteers. The Indians, believing they were being gathered for execution, began an offensive against the soldiers and volunteers. After fresh troops arrived, the Indians were defeated on June 20, and some 600 were sent to the Siletz Reservation on the northern Oregon coast. Those Indians that did not surrender were hunted down and killed, or sometimes captured. There were approximately 10,000 natives in southwestern Oregon when the white men first arrived thirty years earlier, but only 2,000 survivors were sent to Siletz.

BIG MEADOWS BATTLEFIELD, CURRY COUNTY, OREGON, 1991

Fifty-four white men—Mormons—and about two hundred Paiute Indians massacred the majority of Captain Fancher's party of fifty-six men and sixty-two women and children passing through Utah at Mountain Meadows in the southern part of the state. The Mormons falsely believed the rumors that the Fancher party (from Arkansas) was part of the mob that drove the Saints from Missouri and were committing depredations in Utah. After the Fancher train passed through Cedar City, a Church council was held, and it was decided by a unanimous vote to be the will of the Lord that the Fancher party should be executed. The manner selected was an Indian massacre, and so the Indians were enlisted with the promise of loot. It was unquestionably the intention of the Mormon Church to keep the participation of the white men in the massacre a secret, and to lay the blame on the Indians. One hundred and twenty-one people of Fancher's party were killed at Mountain Meadows. Seventeen children survived and were divided out among Mormon families.

—Paraphrased from *Massacres of the Mountains* by J. P. Dunn (New York: Archer House, 1886), pp. 254–67.

I have made that matter a subject of prayer. I went right to God with it, and asked him to take the horrid vision from my sight, if it were a righteous thing that my people had done in killing those people at the Mountain Meadows. God answered me, and at once the vision was removed. I have evidence from God that he has overruled it all for good, and the action was a righteous one and well intended. The brethren acted from pure motives. The only trouble is that they acted a little prematurely; they were a little ahead of time. I sustain you and all of the brethren for what they did.

—Brigham Young, Mormon prophet and leader, from *Massacres of the Mountains* by J. P. Dunn, Jr. (New York: Archer House, 1886), p. 264.

Mountain Meadows Massacre Site, Washington County, Utah, 1988

By 1860 the emigrants traveling the Overland Trail through Utah and Nevada had killed most of the available game, and their stock had left the country barren of plant life. Without their traditional food supply the Goshiute, Shoshoni, and Paiute Indians were reduced to begging or raiding the white emigrants. In response, U.S. troops were sent out from Camp Douglas in Salt Lake City to counter Indian raids along the route west of the Great Salt Lake. In one encounter at Simpson Springs Station these troops surrounded and slaughtered an entire camp of Goshiute men, women, and children. The Goshiute War resulted in the deaths of sixteen whites and over a hundred Indians, and the Overland Trail and the Pony Express route were closed for extended periods from 1860 to 1863.

SIMPSON SPRINGS STATION MASSACRE SITE, TOOELE COUNTY, UTAH, 1990

Two battles were fought at Pyramid Lake in May and June of 1860. These battles started the Paiute resistance to the white invasion of their lands. During the course of the war the Paiutes were driven from their home at Pyramid Lake and were pursued throughout northern Nevada by U.S. troops and volunteers. The Paiutes were subdued and scattered out to reservations in Nevada and Oregon. After the Bannock War of 1878, the Malheur Reservation in Oregon (where most of the Nevada Paiutes were detained) was dissolved, and the Paiutes living there were transferred to the Yakima Reservation in Washington and it wasn't until 1883 that they were allowed to return to Pyramid Lake.

I dreamt this same thing for three nights—the very same. I saw the greatest emigration that has yet been through our country. I looked North and South and East and West, and saw nothing but dust, and I heard a great weeping. I saw women crying, and I also saw my men shot down by the white people. They were killing my people with something that made a great noise like thunder and lightning, and I saw the blood streaming from the mouths of my men that lay all around me. I saw it as if it was real. I feel that it will come to pass.

—Winnemucca, Paiute, from *As Long as the River Shall Run: An Ethnohistory of Pyramid Lake Indian Reservation* by Martha C. Knack and Omer C. Stewart (Berkeley: University of California Press, 1984), p. 37.

Pyramid Lake Battlefield, Pyramid Lake Reservation, Nevada, 1988

The early 1860s witnessed increased American expansion into the Territory of New Mexico. The newcomers encountered fierce resistance from the Apaches and Navajos. The U.S. Army decided that the most effective way to control these tribes was to place them on military reservations under guard. This policy gave birth to Fort Sumner and the Bosque Redondo Reservation.

Troops under the command of Christopher (Kit) Carson invaded the Mescalero Apache and Navajo homelands in 1862 and 1863. The soldiers destroyed their homes, crops, and livestock and the Indians were starved into submission. The captives were forced to march to Fort Sumner, in some cases a distance of over four hundred miles. By the fall of 1864, 500 Apaches and nearly 9,000 Navajos were held at Bosque Redondo.

Despite the best efforts of both the military and Indians, the reservation experiment became a nightmarish catastrophe. Crops were destroyed in turn by cutworms, drought, and hail. Wood was scarce and even the water of the Pecos seemed unhealthy. In 1868, after five years of deprivation, the captives were allowed to return to their homelands where they remain today.

—From *New Mexico State Monuments,* an informational brochure published by the State of New Mexico.

SITE OF THE APACHE AND NAVAJO CAPTIVITY, BOSQUE REDONDO, FORT SUMNER, NEW MEXICO, 1991

On September 3, 1862, in the campaign to punish the Santee Sioux for the Sioux Uprising of 1862, General Alfred Sully came upon a camp of 3,500 Yanktonai, Huncpapa, and Santee Sioux at Whitestone Hill in eastern North Dakota. The Huncpapa and Yanktonai were not at war with the government. Sully attacked the camp, and an estimated 150 Indians were killed. The Sioux fled, abandoning their lodges and 100,000 pounds of buffalo meat. The Huncpapa (Sitting Bull's people) were alienated by this indiscriminate attack and their hostility toward and distrust of U.S. forces dates from this battle.

WHITESTONE HILL BATTLEFIELD, WHITESTONE BATTLEFIELD HISTORIC SITE, NORTH DAKOTA, 1989

The Battle of Bear River was fought in this vicinity January 29, 1863. Colonel P. E. Connor leading 300 California Volunteers from Camp Douglas, Utah, against Bannock and Shoshone Indians guilty of hostile attacks on emigrants and settlers, engaged about 500 Indians, of whom 250–300 were killed or incapacitated, including 90 combatant women and children. Fourteen soldiers were killed, 4 officers and 49 men were wounded, of whom 1 officer and 7 men died later. Seventy-nine were severely frozen. Chiefs Bear Hunter, Sagwitch, and Lehi were reported killed. One hundred seventy-five horses and much stolen property were recovered. Seventy lodges were burned.

—Words on the monument at Bear River Massacre Site. Erected 1932 by Franklin County Daughters of the Utah Pioneers, Cache Valley Council of the Boy Scouts of America, and Utah Pioneer Trails and Landmarks Association.

Very few Indians survived an attack here when P. E. Connor's California Volunteers trapped and destroyed a band of Northwestern Shoshoni.

Friction between local Indians and white travelers along this route led Connor to set out on a cold winter campaign. More than 400 Shoshoni occupied a winter camp that offered ideal protection in Battle Creek Canyon. But they suffered a military disaster unmatched in western history when Connor's force struck at daybreak on January 29, 1863.

—New Marker at the Bear River Massacre Site, erected late 1980s.

BEAR RIVER MASSACRE SITE, FRANKLIN COUNTY, IDAHO, 1991

On November 29, 1864, Black Kettle's band of peaceful Cheyennes was attacked by the Third Colorado Volunteers under the command of Colonel John M. Chivington. The soldiers mutilated the dead and brought back to Denver over a hundred Indian scalps, which were exhibited between shows of a theatrical performance. According to George Bent, at least 137 people were murdered with two-thirds of that number being women and children.

"Colorado soldiers have again covered themselves with glory. All acquitted themselves well."—*Rocky Mountain News, December 17, 1864*

In going over the battleground the next day, I did not see a body of man, woman, or child but was scalped; and in many instances their bodies were mutilated in the most horrible manner—men, women, and children—privates cut out, etc; I heard one man say that he had cut a woman's private parts out and had them for exhibition on a stick; I heard another man say that he had cut the fingers off an Indian to get the rings on the hand; according to the best of my knowledge and belief, these atrocities that were committed were with the knowledge of J. M. Chivington, and I do not know of his taking any measures to prevent them; I heard of one instance of a child a few months old being thrown in the feedbox of a wagon, and after being carried some distance, left on the ground to perish; I also heard of numerous instances in which men had cut out the private parts of females, and stretched them over the saddle-bows, and wore them over their hats, while riding in the ranks.

—James D. Connor, First Lieutenant, from *Condition of the Indian Tribes,* Report of the Joint Special Committee on the Chivington Massacre (Washington, D.C.: U.S. Government Printing Office, 1867), p. 53.

SAND CREEK MASSACRE SITE, KIOWA COUNTY, COLORADO, 1987

Although Congressional hearings were held to investigate the massacre at Sand Creek, neither J. M. Chivington nor members of the Colorado Third Volunteers were held accountable for the atrocities they committed.

There was one little child, probably three years old, just big enough to walk through the sand. The Indians had gone ahead, and this little child was behind following after them. The little fellow was perfectly naked, traveling on the sand. I saw one man get off his horse, at a distance of about seventy-five yards, and draw up his rifle and fire—he missed the child. Another man came up and said, "Let me try the son of a bitch; I can hit him." He got down off his horse, kneeled down and fired at the little child, but he missed him. A third man came up and made a similar remark, and fired, and the little fellow dropped.

—Major Scott J. Anthony, from *Massacre of the Cheyenne Indians* (39th U.S. Congress, 2nd Session Senate Report 156, 1867).

SAND CREEK MASSACRE SITE, KIOWA COUNTY, COLORADO, 1987

Red Cloud refused to sign the Treaty of 1866 which would have provided safe passage for whites flocking to the gold fields of Montana over the Bozeman Trail. This trail passed through the heart of the Lakota and Cheyenne hunting grounds in the Powder River County. The battle on Crazy Woman Fork of the Powder River was one of many in Red Cloud's War, including the Wagon Box Fight and the Fetterman Massacre in which the Lakota and Cheyenne wiped out Captain Fetterman and eighty soldiers. The war was concluded with the Treaty of 1868 at Fort Laramie. U.S. troops were pulled out of the region, the Bozeman Trail was abandoned, and Fort Phil Kearney was burned by the Cheyenne.

CRAZY WOMAN BATTLEFIELD, JOHNSON COUNTY, WYOMING, 1987

The Treaty of 1868 ended Red Cloud's War and guaranteed the sacred Black Hills and the Powder River hunting grounds to the Lakota and Cheyenne people. By 1875 white miners were digging for gold in the sacred lands.

COUNCIL GROUNDS AND AGENCY AT FT. LARAMIE, SITE OF THE TREATY OF 1868, GOSHEN COUNTY, WYOMING, 1987

The Black Hills are sacred to the Lakota and Cheyenne people and are part of Lakota treaty land preserved for their undisturbed use by the Fort Laramie Treaty of 1868. In 1980 the U.S. Supreme Court upheld a lower court decision that the Black Hills had been stolen from the Lakota when they were annexed by Congress in 1889. The ruling said: "A more ripe and rank case of dishonorable dealing will never be found in the history of our country." The Lakota were awarded $122 million in compensation, which was a fraction of the $1 billion in gold taken out of the Homestake Mine. The traditional Oglala Lakotas refused the money and insisted on the return of their sacred land. In 1987 Senator Bill Bradley proposed legislation to return to the Lakota all existing federal land in the Black Hills. The bill died in Congress.

Wherever we went, the soldiers came to kill us, and it was all our own country. It was ours already when Wasichus made the treaty with Red Cloud [Fort Laramie Treaty of 1868], that said it would be ours as long as the grass should grow and water flow. That was only eight winters before, and they were chasing us now because we remembered and they forgot. . . .

We camped on the Tongue River where there was some cottonwood for the ponies; and a hard winter came on early. It snowed much; game was hard to find, and it was a hungry time for us. Ponies died, and we ate them. There had been thousands of us together that summer, but there were not two thousand now.

News came to us there in the Moon of the Falling Leaves that the Black Hills had been sold to Wasichus and also all the country west of the Hills—the country we were in then. I learned when I was older that our people did not want to do this. The Wasichus went to some of the chiefs and got them to put their marks on the treaty. Maybe some of them did this when they were crazy from drinking the *minne wakan* the Wasichus gave them. I have heard this; I do not know. But only crazy or very foolish men would sell their Mother Earth. Sometimes I think it might have been better if we had stayed together and made them kill us all.

—Black Elk, Lakota, from *Black Elk Speaks* by John G. Neihardt (Lincoln: University of Nebraska Press, 1932), pp. 134–35.

Black Hills, Sacred Ground, Custer County, South Dakota, 1989

In October of 1867 over 4,000 Indians—Comanches, Kiowas, Kiowa-Apaches, Southern Arapahoes, and Southern Cheyennes—met with U.S. commissioners to negotiate peace on the southern plains. According to white newspaper correspondents on the scene, it was doubtful that the Indians understood that they were giving up a vast territory for small reservations in Oklahoma. The peace was short-lived as warriors continued to raid north, and in retaliation Custer attacked the sleeping village of Black Kettle's Cheyennes on the Washita River in November of 1868. This was the same Black Kettle whose people were massacred at Sand Creek almost four years to the day earlier. Then in violation of the Medicine Lodge Treaty, white buffalo hunters invaded the southern treaty lands igniting the War to Save the Buffalo.

My people have never first drawn a bow or fired a gun against the whites. There has been trouble on the line between us, and my young men have danced the war-dance. But it was not begun by us. It was you to send the first soldier and we who sent out the second. Two years ago I came upon this road, following the buffalo, that my wives and children might have their cheeks plump and their bodies warm. But the soldiers fired on us, and since that time there has been a noise like that of a thunderstorm, and we have not known which way to go. So it was upon the Canadian.

Nor have we been made to cry once alone. The blue dressed soldiers and the Utes came from out of the night when it was dark and still, and for campfires they lit our lodges. Instead of hunting game they killed my braves, and the warriors of the tribe cut short their hair for the dead. So it was in Texas. They made sorrow come into our camps, and we went out like the buffalo bulls when the cows are attacked. When we found them, we killed them, and their scalps hang in our lodges.

The Comanches are not weak and blind, like the pups of the dog when seven sleeps old. They are strong and far-sighted, like grown horses. We took their road and went on it. The white women cried and our women laughed.

But there are things which you have said to me that I do not like. They were not sweet like sugar, but bitter like gourds. You said that you wanted to put us on a reservation, to build our houses and make us medicine lodges. I do not want them. I was born upon the prairie where the wind blew free and there was nothing to break the light of the sun.

If Texans had kept out of my country there might have been peace. But that which you say we must live on is too small. The Texans have taken away the places where the grass grew the thickest and the timber the best. Had we kept that, we might have done the things you ask. But it is too late. The white man has the country which we loved, and we only wish to wander on the prairies until we die.

—Ten Bears, Comanche, excerpt from his speech at the Medicine Lodge Treaty Council, 1867

MEDICINE LODGE TREATY SITE, BARBER COUNTY, KANSAS, 1988

A border ruffian, a white man named Clark, had assaulted a young Indian, beating him severely, and the Indian, in retaliation, had killed Clark and gone off into Canada. Without troubling to find the guilty party, or even the band he belonged to, Brevet Col. E. M. Baker, Major, Second Cavalry, stationed at Fort Shaw, marched out, under orders from Gen. Philip H. Sheridan, to the nearest Indian village, on Marias River; as it happened they were peaceable, friendly Indians, under Bear's Head. Without warning the soldiers silently surrounded the sleeping village. But the story is better told by Shultz, who was on the spot later, and heard it all from those who saw:

> In a low tone Colonel Baker spoke a few words to his men, telling them to keep cool, aim to kill, to spare none of the enemy; and then he gave the command to fire. A terrible scene ensued. On the previous day many of the men of the camp had gone out toward the Sweetgrass Hills on a grand buffalo hunt; so, save for Chief Bear's Head and a few old men, none were there to return the soldiers fire. Their first volley was aimed low down into the lodges, and many of the sleeping people were killed or wounded in their beds. The rest rushed out, men, children, women, many of the latter with babes in their arms, only to be shot down at the doorways of their lodges. . . . Of the more than 400 souls in the camp at the time, very few escaped. And when it was all over, when the last wounded woman and child had been put out of misery, the soldiers piled the corpses on overturned lodges, firewood, and household property and set fire to it all.

—From an account of the Baker Massacre of the Piegans on January 23, 1870 in *Survey of Conditions of Indians in the United States* (Washington, D.C.: U.S. Government Printing Office, 1930), Part 2.

Marias River Massacre Site (Baker's Massacre of the Piegan Blackfeet), Toole County, Montana, 1990

U.S. troops and Pawnee scouts commanded by Major Eugene A. Carr attacked the raiding Cheyenne Dog Soldier camp of Tall Bull on July 11, 1869. Tall Bull was among the fifty-two Cheyenne killed. Seventeen women and children and over four hundred horses and mules were captured. All the Indian lodges, camp equipment, clothing, and dried meat was burned. The Cheyenne people lost control of their ancestral hunting grounds between the Platte and Arkansas rivers.

SUMMIT SPRINGS BATTLEFIELD, LOGAN COUNTY, COLORADO, 1987

Eskiminzin and about 500 Apaches had surrendered and were living peacefully on Aravaipa Creek about five miles upstream from Camp Grant. On April 30, 1871 William S. Oury led a vigilante force of ninety-two Papago Indians, forty-two Mexicans, and six Anglo-Americans from Tucson to Camp Grant to punish the Indians whom they believed were raiding from the safety of the protection at Camp Grant. The exact number of Apaches killed by this vigilante force is not known; estimates range between 85 and 135. Of the known dead only eight were men. At the trial that followed, even though there was no evidence connecting the Aravaipa Apaches to the alleged depradations that caused the Tucson group to be organized, all the vigilantes were acquitted.

On my arrival I found that I should have but little use for wagon or medicine; the work had been too thoroughly done. The camp had been fired, and the dead bodies of some twenty-one women and children were lying scattered over the ground; those who had been wounded in the first instance had their brains beaten out with stones. Two of the best-looking of the squaws were lying in such a position, and from the appearance of the genital organs and of their wounds, there can be no doubt that they were first ravished and then shot dead. Nearly all of the dead were mutilated. One infant of some ten months was shot twice, and one leg hacked nearly off. While going over the ground, we came upon a squaw who was unhurt, but were unable to get her to come in and talk, she not feeling very sure of our good intentions.

—C. B. Briesly, Camp Grant Post Surgeon (excerpt from his official report filed after the massacre in Aravaipa Canyon), from *Peace with the Apaches of New Mexico and Arizona*, Report of Vincent Colyer (Washington, D.C.: U.S. Government Printing Office, 1872), p. 34.

Captain Jack's Cave, Lava Beds National Monument, California, 1988

During the Apache Wars of 1861 to 1871 this place was the refuge of Cochise and his Chiricahua Apaches. After his death in June of 1874 he was buried in a cave in the stronghold.

When I was young I walked all over this country, east and west, and saw no other people than Apaches. After many summers I walked again and found another race of people had come to take it. . . . The Apaches were once a great nation; they are now but few, and because of this they want to die and so carry their lives on their finger nails. Many have been killed in battle. You must speak straight so that your words may go as sunlight to our hearts. Tell me, if the Virgin Mary has walked throughout all the land, why has she never entered the wigwam of the Apache? Why have we never seen or heard her? . . . I want to live in these mountains; I do not want to go to Tularosa. That is a long ways off. The flies on those mountains eat out the eyes of the horses. The bad spirits live there. I have drunk of these waters and they have cooled me; I do not want to leave here.

—Cochise, Apache, 1871 Peace Council

COCHISE'S STRONGHOLD IN THE DRAGOON MOUNTAINS, COCHISE COUNTY, ARIZONA, 1988

One day the able Mangas Coloradas, chief of the Mimbrenos, made a friendly visit to some gold miners at Pinos Altos in southwestern New Mexico. They tied him up and whipped him unmercifully. Understandably, he went on the war path. Then some Apache band—probably from the Pinal Mountains—captured a twelve-year-old, half-Irish, half-Mexican boy, later known as Mickey Free. Cochise, the chief of the Chiricahuas, had always been friendly to the Anglos; he regularly sold wood to the stage station at the gateway to the tortuous Apache Pass that wound through his mountains. Now a detail of cavalry was sent to demand the stolen boy. With some of his warriors he came unsuspecting to the station to explain that he knew nothing about the captive. The rash young officer in command (Second Lieutenant George N. Bascom, a twenty-five-year-old West Pointer who had been in Arizona only a few months) then seized the Indians, intending to hold them as hostages for the return of the boy. Cochise and three of his men cut a hole in the tent where they were held and escaped. Then he captured some of the stage people and tried without result to exchange prisoners. The dispute ended with Cochise killing his captives and the military hanging theirs. Then Cochise joined with Mangas Coloradas in a war that brought swift-striking Apache death to hundreds of people and devastated a large part of Arizona.

—From *A History of the Indians of the United States* by Angie Debo, Civilization of the American Indian Series, vol. 106 (Norman: University of Oklahoma Press, 1970), pp. 163–64.

Site of the Bascom Affair, Apache Pass, Cochise County, Arizona, 1988

When the decision was made to send the Chiricahua Apache prisoners of war to Florida, they began an odyssey of dislocation and suffering as terrible as any inflicted on American Indians. In Florida the warriors pulled time at Fort Pickens, their families at Fort Marion. The subtropical humidity ravaged the Indians, who were accustomed to the air of desert mountains; perhaps a third of them died there. Some of the children . . . were sent to the famous Indian school at Carlisle, Pennsylvania. . . . In a few years the families were re-united at Mt. Vernon Barracks, Alabama; and in 1894—eight years after the surrender [of Geronimo]—they were removed to Fort Sill, Oklahoma. . . . At Fort Sill many of the older generation passed away.

—From *Apaches: A History and Culture Portrait* by James L. Haley (Garden City, N.Y.: Doubleday and Company, 1981), p. 413.

We are vanishing from the Earth, yet I cannot think we are useless or Usen would not have created us.

For each tribe of men Usen created He also made a home. In the land for any particular tribe He placed whatever would be best for the welfare of that tribe.

When Usen created the Apaches He also created their homes in the West. He gave them such grain, fruits, and game as they needed to eat. To restore their health when disease attacked them He taught them where to find these herbs, and how to prepare them for medicine. He gave them a pleasant climate and all they needed for clothing and shelter was at hand.

Thus it was in the beginning: the Apaches and their homes each created for the other by Usen himself. When they are taken from these homes they sicken and die. How long will it be until it is said there are no more Apaches?

—Geronimo, Apache

Site of the Apache Captivity, Fort Pickens, Gulf Islands National Seashore, Florida, 1991

By the Treaty of 1868 the Black Hills and Powder River regions were recognized as inviolable Indian land by the U.S. Government. But Custer's illegal expedition into the Black Hills in 1874 and the subsequent gold rush forced the Indians to protect their treaty rights. The U.S. government, although bound by treaty to protect Indian lands, decided it was easier and more politically prudent to force the free-roaming Indians onto the reservations than it was to remove the whites from the Black Hills. This round-up campaign of 1876 was commanded by Generals Crook, Gibbon, and Terry, with General Custer under the command of Terry. Custer and his 7th Cavalry arrived first at the large encampment of Lakota and Cheyenne Indians on the Little Bighorn River in eastern Montana. Custer did not wait for Crook, Terry, and Gibbon as planned, but attacked the Indians on June 25, hoping to achieve fame and advancement by defeating the Indians.

In years long-numbered with the past, when I was verging upon manhood, my every thought was ambitious—not to be wealthy, not to be learned, but to be great. I desired to link my name with acts and men, and in such a manner as to be a mark of honor—not only to the present, but to future generations.

—George Armstrong Custer

LITTLE BIGHORN BATTLEFIELD, CUSTER NATIONAL MONUMENT, MONTANA, 1989

Estimates concerning the number of Indians camped on the Little Bighorn River vary from 2,500 to 20,000. According to Evan S. Connell in *Son of the Morning Star,* a figure of 3,000 might be disputed but seems reasonable. In another source, *Centennial Campaign,* the author John S. Gray has arrived at a figure of 7,120 Indian people with 1,780 adult males. The Indians themselves did not know except to say that there were thousands. The total number of soldiers killed was about 265, and the number of Indians killed was difficult to determine but 32 seems to be the accepted figure. Although the Indians won the battle at the Little Bighorn, the American public and the U.S. Army cried out for revenge. The Lakota and Cheyenne were relentlessly pursued, punished, and defeated. In September of 1876, the Lakota under American Horse were defeated at Slim Buttes in South Dakota; Sitting Bull and his Huncpapa Lakota went into exile in Canada during the spring of 1877; the Cheyenne were burned out in their winter village in the Bighorn Mountains in November of 1876 and surrendered in the spring of 1877; and Crazy Horse was murdered in the fall of 1877 after coming in to talk surrender terms at Ft. Robinson, Nebraska.

I was told that after the battle two Cheyenne women came across Custer's body. They knew him, because he had attacked their peaceful village on the Washita. These women said, "You smoked the peace pipe with us. Our chiefs told you that you would be killed if you ever made war on us again. But you would not listen. This will make you hear better." The women each took an awl from their beaded cases and stuck them deep into Custer's ears. Somebody who saw this told me about it. . . . Hundreds of books have been written about this battle by people who weren't there. I was there, but all I remember is one big cloud of dust.

—Good Fox, Lakota, from *In the Spirit of Crazy Horse* by Peter Matthiessen (New York: Viking Press, 1983), p. 170.

LITTLE BIGHORN BATTLEFIELD, CUSTER NATIONAL MONUMENT, MONTANA, 1989

Gold was discovered as a result of Custer's illegal expedition into the Black Hills in 1874. By 1875 many whites had swarmed into the Black Hills following what the Indians called the Thieve's Road. Those Indians who resisted the violation of the Treaty of 1868 and the invasion of their sacred lands were declared by the U.S. to be hostiles. In the spring of 1876 a campaign to round up all the "hostile" Cheyenne and Lakota was begun. The Powder River camp of Box Elder and other Cheyenne headmen was attacked by U.S. troops under J. J. Reynolds. The village was burned and the surviving Cheyenne joined Crazy Horse's Oglala and Sitting Bull's Huncpapa Lakotas and traveled with them to the summer camp on the Little Bighorn River.

POWDER RIVER BATTLEFIELD, POWDER RIVER COUNTY, MONTANA, 1989

After hearing of the attack on the peaceful village of the Cheyenne on Powder River, some of the Cheyenne and Lakota people left the Sioux Reservation to join the free-roaming bands. After the defeat of Custer at the Little Bighorn, U.S. troops were deployed around the reservation to stop the exodus. Fearful that the troops were massing to attack them on the reservation, a large band of Cheyenne under Morning Star left the agency at White River intending to meet up with their relatives in the Powder River country. Troops under Colonel Wesley Merritt attacked the Cheyenne at Warbonnet Creek in northwestern Nebraska. Some of the Cheyenne were turned back to the reservation, but Morning Star was able to escape to the north with about half the people.

WARBONNET BATTLEFIELD, SIOUX COUNTY, NEBRASKA, 1987

On November 25, 1876, 1,100 U.S. troops and Indian scouts commanded by Colonel Ranald S. McKenzie located and attacked the winter village of Northern Cheyenne under Morning Star (Dull Knife). The village consisting of 73 lodges and their contents was destroyed. Almost 500 Indian horses were taken. Twenty-five Indians were found dead on the battlefield, but a much larger number were seriously wounded and died later in the freezing cold. Six soldiers and one Indian scout were killed.

   After the destruction of their village in the Bighorn Mountains, the destitute Northern Cheyenne were forced to surrender at Fort Robinson in Nebraska and at Fort Keogh in Miles City, Montana, in the spring of 1877. Their old way of life was ended and the bitter reservation years began for the Northern Cheyenne people.

MORNING STAR BATTLEFIELD, JOHNSON COUNTY, WYOMING, 1987

The Nez Perce under Chief Joseph covered approximately 1,600 miles in eleven weeks in their attempt to reach sanctuary in Canada. They were forced to surrender on October 5, 1877, in the Bear's Paw Mountains of Montana some forty miles short of their goal. Four hundred eighteen people of the approximately 750 men, women, children, and old people who left Oregon were captured.

At the surrender General Nelson Miles promised that the Indians would be sent to the reservation at Lapwaii, Idaho. Instead the Nez Perce were sent to Oklahoma, where many sickened and died. In the spring of 1885 the Nez Perce that were still living—268—were sent to the Lapwaii Reservation and the Colville Reservation in eastern Washington. From 1855 until he died in 1904 Joseph worked without success to get his people returned to the Wallowa Valley in Oregon.

In the end . . . the war cost the United States $1,873,410.43 not counting the loss of private individuals. The Nez Perce survivors of the struggle, once a rich and self-sufficient people, were made destitute, and thereafter became burdens to the American taxpayer. The Indians had lost their horses, cattle, guns, personal possessions, savings of gold dust and cash, homes, freedom—everything but their honor.

—From *The Nez Perce Indians and the Opening of the Pacific Northwest* by Alvin M. Josephy, Jr. (New Haven: Yale University Press, 1965), p. 633.

Tell General Howard that I know his heart. What he told me before I have in my heart. I am tired of fighting. Our chiefs are killed. Looking Glass is dead. It is the young men who say yes or no. He who led the young men is dead. It is cold and we have no blankets. The little children are freezing to death. My people, some of them have run away to the hills and have no blankets, no food; no one knows where they are—perhaps freezing to death. I want to have time to look for my children and see how many I can find. Maybe I shall find them among the dead. Hear me my chiefs. I am tired; my heart is sick and sad. From where the sun now stands, I will fight no more forever.

—Thunder-Rolling-in-the-Mountains (Chief Joseph), Nez Perce

SITE OF THE SURRENDER OF THE NEZ PERCE, BEAR'S PAW MOUNTAINS, BLAINE COUNTY, MONTANA, 1989

Not understanding the white man's method of waging war, the Nez Perce thought they had left the fighting behind them in Idaho when they arrived at the Big Hole Valley in western Montana in August of 1877. The Nez Perce had avoided a fight at Fort Fizzle, Montana, and it was their understanding that they would be allowed to pass peacefully through Montana on their way to Canada.

The Indians were exhausted after their march through the mountains of Idaho and planned to rest for several days at their traditional camping spot on the Big Hole River. Believing that they would not be attacked in Montana, the Nez Perce posted no camp guards, and on the morning of August 9 the sleeping village was attacked by U.S. troops under the command of Colonel John Gibbon. The Nez Perce suffered their biggest loss of the war, with approximately ninety killed and many more wounded. Twenty-five soldiers were killed and thirty-six wounded. The Indians were able to escape, fleeing toward the newly established Yellowstone National Park and then north to Canada.

BIG HOLE BATTLEFIELD, BIG HOLE NATIONAL BATTLEFIELD, MONTANA, 1990

The Wallowa band of the Nez Perce led by Chief Joseph refused to sell their lands in Oregon. They were given thirty days to move their herds and belongings across the Snake River to the Lapwaii Reservation in Idaho. Some angry young men of the tribe killed some miners in retaliation for murders those miners had committed in the past. U.S. troops were sent out to punish the tribe and in June of 1877 met the Nez Perce in battle at White Bird Canyon. The troops were defeated and the Indians began their long flight to Canada.

If we ever owned the land we own it still, for we never sold it. In the treaty councils the commissioners have claimed that our country had been sold to the Government. Suppose a white man should come to me and say, "Joseph, I like your horses, and I want to buy them." I say to him, "No, my horses suit me, I will not sell them." Then he goes to my neighbor and says to him, "Joseph has some good horses. I want to buy them, but he refuses to sell." My neighbor answers, "Pay me the money, and I will sell you Joseph's horses." The white man returns to me and says, "Joseph, I have bought your horses, and you must let me have them." If we sold our lands to the Government, this is the way they were bought.

—Thunder-Rolling-in-the-Mountains (Chief Joseph), Nez Perce

White Bird Canyon Battlefield, Idaho County, Idaho, 1988

After fleeing confinement and suffering in Indian Territory (Oklahoma) to reach their northern homeland, the Northern Cheyenne under Morning Star (Dull Knife) were finally captured in Nebraska in November of 1878 and were confined at Fort Robinson. After refusing to return to the south in a council in January of 1879, the people—130 men, women, and children—were confined to a small barracks without food, water, or heat. Rather than die like animals in a cage they broke out and were slaughtered in the fields and hills surrounding Fort Robinson. One group of thirty-two ran and hid in the bitter cold for fourteen days and were finally shot by U.S. troops in a cutbank of Warbonnet Creek some forty miles northwest of Fort Robinson; six survived. Of approximately 130 Indians who broke out of the barracks, 64 were killed.

The board attaches no blame to anyone in the Military Service, and in view of all the circumstances of this unfortunate business; of the manifest fact that collision with these Indians and subsequent loss of life was unavoidable; of the evident desire of everyone concerned to carry out the orders of the Government in the most effective and yet humane manner; and of the probability that no one else—of equal experience or judgement—could have done any better, respectfully recommends that no action be taken.

—From "Proceeding of a Board of Officers" convened on January 21, 1879 to investigate the Cheyenne breakout at Fort Robinson. (Records of the U.S. Army Commands, Record Group 98, National Archives, Washington, D.C.)

SITE OF THE CHEYENNE OUTBREAK AND MASSACRE AT FORT ROBINSON, FORT ROBINSON STATE PARK, NEBRASKA, 1989

Of the same scale as the figures at Mt. Rushmore, this statue of Crazy Horse is in the beginning stages. The builders of this monument, Ziolkowski Heritage, Inc., claim to have Native American endorsement for this project.

I was not hostile to the white men. We had buffalo for food, and their hides for clothing and for our tipis. We preferred hunting to a life of idleness on the reservation, where we were driven against our will. At times we did not get enough to eat, and we were not allowed to leave the reservation to hunt.

We preferred our own way of living. We were no expense to the government. All we wanted was peace and to be let alone. Soldiers were sent out in the winter, who destroyed our villages.

Then Long Hair [Custer] came in the same way. They say we massacred him, but he would have done the same thing to us had we not defended ourselves and fought to the last. Our first impulse was to escape with women and children, but we were so hemmed in we had to fight.

After that I went up on the Tongue River with a few of my people and lived in peace. But the government would not let me alone. Finally I came back to the Red Cloud Agency. Yet I was not allowed to remain quiet.

I was tired of fighting. I went to the Spotted Tail Agency and asked that chief and his agent to let me live there in peace. I came here with the agent to talk to the Big White Chief but was not given a chance. They tried to confine me. I tried to escape, and a soldier ran this bayonet into me. I have spoken.

—Crazy Horse, Lakota, his dying statement after being stabbed at Fort Robinson, Nebraska

CRAZY HORSE MOUNTAIN, BLACK HILLS, CUSTER COUNTY, SOUTH DAKOTA, 1989

Carlisle Indian School was established in 1879 by General Richard H. Pratt and operated under a policy of forced deculturization, with militaristic rules and harsh discipline. Indian children were forcibly taken from their homes, mainly in the West and Midwest, and sent to Carlisle. Many died there from disease and suicide. In 1894 Congress passed a law forbidding the sending of Indian children to schools outside the state or territory of their residence. Congress also forbade the common practice of withholding rations from tribes who tried to keep their children at home. Carlisle Indian School was closed in 1918.

One day they selected a few boys and told us we were to learn trades. I was to be a tinsmith. I did not care for this, but I tried my best to learn this trade. . . . I made hundreds of tin cups, coffee pots and buckets. These were sent away and issued to the Indians on various reservations. After I left school and returned home, this trade did not benefit me any, as the Indians had plenty of tinware that I made at school.

—From "First Days at Carlisle," in *My People, the Sioux* by Luther Standing Bear (Cambridge, Mass.: Riverside Press; New York: Houghton Mifflin Company, 1928), p. 147.

CARLISLE INDIAN SCHOOL, NOW U.S. ARMY WAR COLLEGE, CARLISLE, PENNSYLVANIA, 1991

With a band of his Huncpapa Lakota, Sitting Bull escaped to Canada in the spring of 1877. In July of 1881 they returned to the United States and surrendered at Fort Buford, North Dakota. They were taken to Fort Randall as prisoners of war and later released to Standing Rock Reservation in South Dakota. Because of his influence with the people and his participation in the Ghost Dance Movement in 1890, Sitting Bull was ordered arrested, and on December 15, he and his son were killed while "resisting arrest."

I wish all to know that I do not propose to sell any part of my country, nor will I have the whites cutting our timber along the rivers, more especially the oak. I am particularly fond of the little groves of oak trees. I love to look at them, because they endure the wintry storm and the summer's heat, and—not unlike ourselves—seem to flourish by them.

—Sitting Bull, Lakota

SITE OF THE SURRENDER OF SITTING BULL AND HIS PEOPLE, FORT BUFORD, WILLIAMS COUNTY, NORTH DAKOTA, 1989

In 1877 the United States and Canada border was the destination of the Nez Perce in their flight from their homeland in Oregon after the Wallowa Valley was stolen. After fleeing and fighting for eleven weeks and having covered 1,600 miles, they were forced to surrender to U.S. troops at Bear's Paw Mountains, some forty miles short of their goal.

The Bannocks of Idaho attempted to reach Canada in 1878 but were also caught before reaching the border.

Sitting Bull and his Huncpapa Lakotas found sanctuary in Canada for four years, from May of 1877 until their surrender to U.S. forces at Fort Buford in July of 1881.

MEDICINE LINE, U.S./CANADA BORDER AT WILDHORSE CHECKPOINT, MONTANA/ALBERTA, 1989

Wovoka was born in 1858. As a young man Wovoka traveled throughout Oregon and Washington where he came into contact with new religions that had sprung up in the Pacific Northwest. In 1886, returning home to Mason Valley, Nevada, he revived his father's old ghost dance with the new influence of the Dreamers, Shakers, Blowers, and Christianity. Wovoka claimed that if the Indians performed the ghost dance faithfully, God would renew the world and remove the white people. Many Indians believed Wovoka to be the Messiah and came from near and far to hear his words and to learn the dance. By 1889 the ghost dance had spread to the plains tribes, where the dancing culminated in the Wounded Knee Massace. After Wounded Knee and owing to the fact that the world stayed the same, enthusiasm for the ghost dance faded and Wovoka died in obscurity in 1932. He is buried in the Indian cemetery near Shurz, Nevada.

Father, have pity on me,
Father, have pity on me.
I am crying for thirst,
I am crying for thirst.
All is gone—I have nothing to eat,
All is gone—I have nothing to eat.

Arapahoe Ghost Dance song

BIRTHPLACE OF WOVOKA, INDIAN MESSIAH AND FOUNDER OF THE GHOST DANCE, MASON VALLEY, NEVADA, 1988

By 1890 Wovoka's Ghost Dance had spread to the tribes of the Great Plains. The Lakota were dancing for renewal at secluded sites all over their reservations. The white reservation authorities were nervous that the dancing would lead to full-scale revolt and warfare. The dance was outlawed, troops were called in, and attempts to stop the Ghost Dance culminated in the killing of Sitting Bull and shortly after that the 7th Cavalry massacred Big Foot and his people at Wounded Knee.

The Whites are crazy!
The Whites are crazy!

Lakota Ghost Dance song

GHOST DANCE SITE IN THE BADLANDS, PINE RIDGE RESERVATION, SOUTH DAKOTA, 1989

On December 29, 1890, while U.S. troops were disarming Big Foot's band of Minneconjou Lakota, a young warrior named Black Coyote fired his rifle. Some accounts say he was deaf and did not understand what was taking place. The 7th Cavalry immediately opened fire on the gathered Indians with rifles and Hotchkiss guns, and the killing was indiscriminate. When the killing stopped, Big Foot and more than half his people were dead. One hundred fifty-three were known dead, but many of the wounded died afterward in the blizzard that followed. One estimate placed the total of dead at almost 300 of the original 350 men, women, and children of Big Foot's band. There were 25 soldiers killed and 39 wounded, mostly by their own bullets as the majority of the Indians had been disarmed. In this, the last "battle" of the Indian wars, the 7th Cavalry took revenge for the killing of Custer when he attacked the village on the Little Bighorn River.

Dead and wounded women and children and little babies were scattered all along where they had been trying to run away. The soldiers had followed along the gulch, as they ran, and murdered them in there. Sometimes they were in heaps because they had huddled together, and some were scattered all along. Sometimes bunches of them had been killed and torn to pieces where the wagon-guns hit them. I saw a little baby trying to suck its mother, but she was bloody and dead. . . . Men and women and children were heaped and scattered all over the flat at the bottom of the little hill where the soldiers had their wagon-guns, and westward up the dry gulch all the way to the high ridge, the dead women and babies were scattered.

. . . And so it was all over. I did not know then how much was ended. When I look back now from this high hill of my old age, I can still see the butchered women and children lying heaped and scattered all along the crooked gulch as plain as when I saw them with eyes still young. And I can see that something else died there in the bloody mud, and was buried in the blizzard. A people's dream died there. It was a beautiful dream.

—Black Elk, Lakota, account of the Wounded Knee Massacre, from *Black Elk Speaks* by John G. Neihardt (Lincoln: University of Nebraska Press), pp. 265–66, 276.

MASS GRAVE AT THE WOUNDED KNEE MASSACRE SITE, PINE RIDGE RESERVATION, SOUTH DAKOTA, 1989

My grandmother had a reverence for the sun, a holy regard that now is all but gone out of mankind. There was a wariness in her, and an ancient awe. She was a Christian in her later years, but she had come a long way about, and she never forgot her birthright. As a child she had been to the Sun Dances; she had taken part in those annual rites, and by them she had learned the restoration of her people in the presence of Tai-me. She was about seven when the last Kiowa Sun Dance was held in 1887 on the Washita River above Rainy Mountain Creek. The buffalo were gone. In order to consummate the ancient sacrifice—to impale the head of a buffalo bull upon the medicine tree—a delegation of old men journeyed into Texas, there to beg and barter for an animal from the Goodnight herd. She was ten when the Kiowas came together for the last time as a living Sun Dance culture. They could find no buffalo; they had to hang an old hide from the sacred tree. Before the dance could begin, a company of soldiers rode out from Fort Sill under orders to disperse the tribe. Forbidden without cause the essential act of their faith, having seen the wild herds slaughtered and left to rot upon the ground, the Kiowas backed away forever from the medicine tree. That was July 20, 1890, at the great bend of the Washita. My grandmother was there. Without bitterness, and for as long as she lived, she bore a vision of deicide.

—N. Scott Momaday, Kiowa, from *The Way to Rainy Mountain* (Albuquerque: University of New Mexico Press, 1969), pp. 9–11.

Site of the Last Kiowa Sun Dance, Great Bend of the Washita River, Custer/Kiowa Counties, Oklahoma, 1990

Minnesota's most recent Indian battle took place in 1898 at Sugar Point on the east shore of Leech Lake. A United States Marshal, who had been sent out to bring back a Chippewa Indian named Hole-in-the-Day to testify in a federal case against illicit liquor dealers, met with resistance. Hole-in-the-Day refused to go, saying that the previous year he had been taken to Duluth as a witness in a similar case and after testifying had been turned loose to walk home, a distance of over a hundred miles.

The marshal immediately ordered the agency police to arrest the Indian, but seventeen of his friends subsequently rescued him. Federal troops were then called out to take the whole group of Indians into custody. General Bacon who had recently returned from service in Cuba, crossed the lake from Walker to Sugar Point with a detachment of the regular army. When the soldiers landed, the Indians fired a volley and then shoved the boats from the beach as the detachment ran for cover. Major Wilkinson and six privates were killed in the battle that followed, while the Indians registered no casualties. Hole-in-the-Day was not arrested.

—From *Minnesota, Federal Writer's Project* (St. Clair's Shores, Minn.: Somerset Publishers, 1976), Tour 20, p. 60.

Leech Lake Battlefield, Sugar Point, Cass County, Minnesota, 1991

Palus was located at the confluence of the Palouse and Snake rivers. A few Palouse people continued to live at the village until the mid-twentieth century when the land was condemned to allow the construction of the Ice Harbor Dam. The waters of Lake Sacajawea covered the village site and the graves of the Palouse. It is now the site of a Washington state park.

They say we are extinct, but we are not.

—Karie Jim Nightwalker, Palouse, from *Renegade Tribe: The Palouse Indians and the Invasion of the Inland Pacific Northwest* by Clifford E. Trafzer and Richard D. Scheurman (Pullman: Washington State University Press, 1986), p. 137.

SITE OF THE LAST VILLAGE OF THE PALOUSE PEOPLE AT PALUS, COLUMBIA/WHITMAN COUNTIES, WASHINGTON, 1989

Haunted America

Patricia Nelson Limerick

TALES FROM HELL

. . . you will soon find it theologically and factu-
ally true that man by nature is a damn mess.
Norman Maclean
A River Runs Through It

Drex Brooks has traveled thousands of miles to photograph the sites of treaty negotiations, forced migrations, battles, and massacres.

I wish I knew why.

When I agreed to write this essay, I thought I did
know.* Brooks, I believed (and I may actually have
been right), had taken up this draining and demanding enterprise because he wanted us to face the facts
of our national history. With these photographs,
Brooks wanted to make his contemporaries recognize that our very presence on this continent rests
on a foundation of violent conquest. Americans have
grown fond of an image of themselves as a nation of
innocents. Drex Brooks wanted to offer a different
set of images, putting that presumption of innocence to a critical inspection. In North America,
just as much as in South America, Africa, Asia, and
Australia, Europeans invaded a land fully occupied
by natives. Sometimes by negotiation and sometimes
by warfare, the natives lost ground and the invaders
gained it. From the caves in the Lava Beds of northern California, where the Modocs held off the United
States Army for months, to the site along the Mystic
River in Connecticut where Puritans burned Pequots trapped in a stockade, the landscape bears
witness to the violent subordination of Indian people. These haunted locations are not distant, exotic

*I am much indebted to my student Mike Uihlein who took part in
this exploration with me; as a Wisconsinite and veteran member of
the Black Hawks football team, Mike finally found out who Black
Hawk was and what happened at Bad Axe. I am very grateful, as well, to
the teachers in the National Endowment for the Humanities Institute
on the American West in the summer of 1993, for helping me think.

sites set apart from the turf of our normal lives. Neither time nor space can insulate us from these unsettling histories.

At the beginning, then, I had my part in this project figured out. I would do in words what Brooks was doing in the photographs. Photograph or paragraph, the components of this book would carry the same message: "Look at these places. Think about what happened here. Recognize the chain of events that connects these acts of invasion and conquest to your presence here today."

So that was what I set out to write: a text that would ground the big picture of conquest in the stories of these particular places.

And then, the next thing I knew, I was standing at the point of a head-on collision, where this simple plan ran into the maddening complexity of the stories of war.

In terms of simplicity and complexity, one can draw an exact analogy between the idea of the Rocky Mountains and the idea of conquest. Everyone knows that a big range of mountains divides the continent, running from Mexico to Canada. When you approach the Rockies from the Plains and you glimpse a wall of mountains in the distance, you can say with clarity and precision, "Those are the Rocky Mountains up ahead."

But go past the plains, past the foothills, and into the mountains themselves, and neither clarity nor precision remains an option. What you have in front of you—more to the point, what you are immersed in—is a labyrinth, a sprawl of peaks and valleys and parks and meadows and canyons in no discernible pattern. This is not a mountain range. This is a mountain jumble, and it extends for hundreds of miles.

Consider the Rockies from a distance, and they are a clearly marked range of mountains separating the Great Plains from the Columbia Plateau, the Great Basin, and the southwestern deserts. But place yourself, instead, in the midst of the Rockies themselves, and that clear line of mountains becomes a maze and a muddle.

In the same way, if you place yourself at a distance, then there is no clearer fact in American history than the fact of conquest. The land was occupied by Indian people; whites entered as invaders; as soon as the whites wanted permanent possession of the land, they drove the Indians from their homes, sometimes with treaties and negotiations, oftentimes with pure force. When you stand at a distance, this proposition appears in stark outline: Europeans and their descendants took North America from Indians, and took it with violence.

But surrender that distance, and immerse yourself in the story of the dispossession of any one group, and clarity dissolves. There is nothing linear or direct in these stories. Only in rare circumstances were the affairs that we call "white/Indians wars" only matters of whites against Indians. More often, Indians took part on both sides, tribe against tribe or faction against faction, with whites sometimes playing surprisingly peripheral roles in the working out of relationships between and among Indian groups. And, if Indians were often divided against each other, the same shortage of solidarity applied to the other side. In the tense and unpredictable circumstances before, during, and after a war, whites often squabbled bitterly with each other, presenting something one would not begin to call a united front.

In virtually every case, the story of how the war got started is a long, detailed, and tangled business. These are narratives designed to break the self-esteem of storytellers. You can be the world's greatest enthusiast for narrative history, and you can still lose your nerve at the prospect of putting yourself and your readers at the mercy of one of these tales from hell.

They are tales from hell because they are stories so loaded with tiresome detail and pointless plot twists that narrative art bends and breaks under their weight. They are tales from hell, as well, because they are stories that drive their tellers and readers to a confrontation with the darkest and grimmest dimensions of human nature. Torture, maiming, rape, mutilation, murder: all of the worst injuries that human beings inflict on each other serve as the capstones to these stories. Whites did these things to Indians, and Indians did these things to whites. Invaded or invader, conquered or conqueror, nearly every group had occasion to use terror as a memorable method of communication.

The person who contemplates these tales ends up feeling a kind of nondiscriminatory moral shock, unnerved by nearly everybody's behavior. Of course, one can never lose sight of who started the whole business. Indians never invaded Europe; Indian tribes did not cross the Atlantic to seize the homes, fields, and sacred places of Europeans. It is perfectly clear who started this fight. And it is also perfectly clear who, when the dust had settled, had maneuvered whom into surrendering land, food, and the weapons of aggression and self-defense. But in between those two points of clarity lies a great stretch of historical turf in which people of all ethnicities and backgrounds embraced brutality and committed atrocities. In this disorienting turf, neither victims nor villains come with consistent labeling.

In the muddled events that lie between the beginning of invasion and the invaders' consolidated domination, historical lessons are hard to come by. "Morals of the story" that lift the spirit and inspire hope simply do not appear. On some occasions, historians are quick to make cheerful remarks about how the understanding of history will help us to understand ourselves and to cope with the dilemmas we have inherited from the past. It is hard to pipe up with one of those earnest declarations of faith in the value of historical knowledge, when you are thinking of the water at the junction of the Mississippi River and the Bad Axe River (Fig. 1). That water, on August 2, 1832, was reddened with the blood of the wounded Sauk and Fox people trying to escape the bullets of American troops. In Indian agent Joseph

Figure 1. Bad Axe Battlefield

Street's description, "The Inds. were pushed literally into the Mississippi, the current of which was at one time perceptibly tinged with the blood of the Indians who were shot on its margin & in the stream. . . . It is impossible to say how many Inds. have been killed, as most of them were shot in the water or drowned in attempting to cross the Mississippi."[1] Those Indians who survived the crossing at Bad Axe did not leave brutality behind them when they escaped from the white soldiers. The survivors were attacked a few days later—by a party of Sioux.

What good can knowledge of this miserable story do? Is the principal lesson simply that the "Winning of Illinois" was as tangled, brutal, and bloody a process as the "Winning of Massachusetts" or the "Winning of Oregon"? What exactly does knowledge of this event add to American self-understanding—and well-being?

When I went to college, I had a fine professor in my freshman course in Western Civilization. Jasper Rose was from England, and given to the use of terms of address like "ducky." One day in class, we talked about the Calvinist belief in the evil that had lodged in the human soul after the fall of Adam. The way that Mr. Rose had discussed the topic of human depravity puzzled me to my core.

"When you were talking about the way people used to believe in the evil in humans," I said to him after class, "you sounded as if *you* believed there is such a thing. But how could a modern person believe in human depravity?"

"Just wait, ducky," Mr. Rose sighed. "Just wait."

Jasper Rose, it seems to me now, was doing his best to get me braced for the Battle of Bad Axe. But there is no way to be truly braced for the dreadful reality of the events that took place on the sites that Drex Brooks has photographed. The Mystic Fort Fire, the Ohio River Wars, Black Hawk's War, the Mountain Meadows Massacre, the Bear River Massacre, the Sand Creek Massacre, the Modoc War, and the Nez Perce War, to name a few: all these events have me flummoxed. They are the most miserable stories I have read in a long time. I remember how clear things seemed when I thought I understood Drex Brooks's motives for asking that we bring these events back into our common memory. Now, after living for a while with little else on my mind, I cannot understand why Brooks took up this project, nor how he stayed with it for years. Yes, these stories are part of our national heritage; yes, they shaped us as a people; yes, we have to know our past to understand our present. But, by remembering these stories, what do we gain besides a revival and restoration of the misery?

Some readers will see considerable irony in the path of these reflections. I am the author of a book called *The Legacy of Conquest.* We must, I said in that book, we must look clearly and directly at the workings of conquest and cease to hide the rough reality of western history behind the fuzzy concept of the "frontier." In the judgment of some historians and a number of journalists, the vision recorded in *Legacy* is a dark and grim one. My school of western history, a historian of a brighter vision has written, concentrates on the "dark strains" and "splatters of mud," offering "a picture of unrelieved bleakness," "a somber West, devoid of light, marked by hardship, suffering and failure" and peopled by "victims of institutionalized brutality and avarice." Another historian finds the explanation of my grimness in my birthdate: "Like many historians of the 1960s generation, she reflected the negativism and disdain for previous interpretations." Limerick, the description goes on, "chronicled what she perceived as a shameful legacy of conquest. In her account of the forming of the West, the record was one of unmitigated suppression, of women, of Native Americans, of blacks, and of Hispanics, not to speak of wanton despoliation and destruction of the natural environment." As evidence in support of this characterization, my critic cites the entire text of *The Legacy of Conquest,* with every page heavy with sorrow and shame.[2]

While I have been reading descriptions of my grim and dark vision for several years now, the fact is that there are few people who can match my belief in the therapeutic power of history and in the social glue that comes from the exercise of empathy. I have been a committed and audible holder of the faith that the calm and careful exploration of our common history is our best route to peaceful living in the present. The last sentences of *The Legacy of Conquest* record a faith that would seem hard to characterize as "dark," "bleak," "grim," or full of "shame":

"Indians, Hispanics, Asians, blacks, Anglos, businesspeople, workers, politicians, bureaucrats, natives, and newcomers, we share the same region and its history, but we wait to be introduced. The serious exploration of the historical process that made us neighbors provides that introduction."[3] With that conclusion, I went on record as a relic believer in an embattled and besieged optimism—an optimism so embattled and besieged that it is easy to imagine my future as an exhibit in a museum. "Patricia Nelson Limerick, a historian who lived in Boulder, Colorado," the exhibit label will read, "was one of the last believers in the proposition that human beings who understood their common past could live in peace with each other."

Perhaps, then, a better route to testing the proposition that *The Legacy of Conquest* is a depressing and "negative" book, is to ask the question, "How were white/Indian wars presented in the book? Did Limerick dwell on the wars in order to exaggerate and overemphasize the grimness of the Western past?"

The answer to the question gives the game away. There are no white/Indian wars in *Legacy.* This was not a matter of accident. Reading the manuscript, one of my editors raised the question, "Where are the Plains Wars? Where are *any* Indian wars?" The wars are not in the book, I told him, because tribes who never fought the United States Army ended up conquered and placed on reservations, anyway. The wars may have caught popular imagination, but they were not the key element in conquest.

There is some logic to that answer, but I suspect I turned to it to mask a more truthful answer. "I am leaving the wars out," the more honest answer would have run, "because I am leaving out the ugliest parts of this story. I would like this book to provide a basis for collaboration and reconciliation for today's Westerners. If I tell the full story of the violence of conquest, I will destroy any possible foundation for reconciliation."

And so, seven years ago, I successfully weaseled out of the obligation to face up to the white/Indian wars. But there is no escape from history. Here, thanks to Drex Brooks and his photographs, are the wars and massacres, back for a reckoning.

But by making this reckoning, what does one do but revive the misery? Why insist that your contemporaries contemplate the details of bodies with their surfaces and interiors broken by bullets, arrows, and knives? If you demand that people pay attention to these disheartening stories, can you really pass this demand off as public service?

THE SHARP POINT OF CONQUEST

If there be one principle more deeply rooted than any other in the mind of every American, it is that we should have nothing to do with conquest.
Thomas Jefferson, letter to William Short, 1791

The United States is stained with the blood drawn by conquest.

Indian people have recognized this fact for several centuries. European colonists and American pioneers, for that matter, understood that their acquisition of territory rested on wars fought to displace the natives. Settlers who petitioned for troops to defeat and remove the local Indian population publicly surrendered their faith in the proposition that America was a virgin land, free, open, and eager for inhabitation by Europeans and their descendants. In the nineteenth century, a surprising number of white Americans spoke and wrote with sympathy for the natives, recognizing the Indians' reasons for defending their homelands and lamenting the brutality of white American responses to native resistance. In the twentieth century, the end of armed Indian resistance permitted white Americans to indulge in waves of admiration for the nobility of the defeated natives and of regret for the injuries committed against them. A ritualized sigh over "what we did to the Indians" had become a standard element of popular American culture.

In the 1990s, an awareness of the injuries of conquest could wear just about any label but "new." Many Americans recognize that their prosperity rests on the violent displacement of Indian people.

But does this make any difference?

Judging from these photographs, the answer seems to be "No." Drex Brooks has photographed sites where the broad process of conquest once came to a sharp focus. Most of the people who appear here, in person or represented by their acts and works, seem pleasantly unaware of the miserable events that took place at these locations. If you go by the evidence of these photographs, people today visit these sites to fish, to play softball, to dump trash, to buy postcards, to herd cattle, to build roads, to park their cars, or to camp. They give few signs of having come to contemplate the violence built into the foundations of American history.

By taking these sites for granted, we have anesthetized ourselves to history. When these places have monuments and markers, they seem less an opportunity for contemplation, and more an opportunity for tourist children, cooped up too long in minivans, to get in some much-needed exercise. Even for visitors with some interest in history, these sites often stand as relics of a colorful, quaint, romantic, and very distant American past. Late-twentieth-century Americans may shudder over the newspaper's story of a murder committed the night before, but the pain of a violent death that occurred more than a century ago comes to us much reduced.

We live, these photographs tell us, in a state of blunted feeling, capable of a cheerful indifference when we visit land once steeped in human agony. Contemplating this indifference can be, at first, infuriating. Americans ought to know what acts of violence bought them their right to own land, build homes, use resources, and travel freely in North America. Americans ought to know what happened on the ground they stand on; they surely have some obligation to know where they are.

Figure 2. Sand Creek

But try this: imagine what it would be like to tell them.

A tour bus driver chats and smokes at the site of the Sand Creek Massacre (Fig. 2). His passengers wonder where on earth they are, how long they will be there, and how much farther it is to Denver. Let us say that I arrive at this moment and seize the opportunity to awaken, in this captive audience, an awareness of history and the prices of conquest.

If this were my opportunity to move the indifferent, then how on earth would I get the long, detailed, maddening story of the Sand Creek Massacre to cooperate? The chain of events leading up to the events of November 29, 1864, is a very complicated one.[4] Telling it accurately and thoroughly would take, I estimate, two hours. This is what I would have to cover: early tribal movements and migrations; traditions of intertribal warfare and the values and aspirations of warriors; the changes brought by the fur trade; the development of stereotypes and images of Indians in Anglo-American minds; the Pike's Peak mining rush; the founding of white settlements at Denver and elsewhere in the Rockies; the creation of territorial government; the personalities, ambitions, and dilemmas of territorial officials; the personalities, ambitions, and dilemmas of Cheyenne and Arapaho leaders; the negotiation of a treaty of questionable legitimacy; the effects of the Civil War on the West; the conflicts between the regular army and civilian volunteer units; the escalating cycle of attacks and retaliations between whites and Indians over Colorado's vulnerable supply line to the eastern United States; and, finally, a torturous chain of communications and miscommunications between and among tribal people, territorial officials, white Coloradans, army officers, and federal agencies in distant Washington, D.C.

So two hours would pass, and I would only have my story up to November 28, 1864, the day before the massacre. My audience of captive tourists, we can safely assume, would be bored and restive. Visits to western historical sites should be fun and colorful, with pleasant family photo opportunities. The history of the Old West is supposed to be romantic and adventurous, but this particular chapter of history is complicated, tiresome, apparently endless, and very dull.

After this point, however, the story cannot be called dull.

Just after dawn, on November 29, 1864, Colonel John Chivington unleashed his troops in an attack on the Cheyenne and Arapaho village at Sand Creek. Some Indian men sized up the situation and went for their arms. A few Indians tried to indicate that they were not hostile. Witnesses described the Cheyenne chief Black Kettle trying to display an American flag and a white flag, and the Arapaho leader White Antelope standing unarmed before the soldiers, simply singing his death song. Women and children scattered, trying to escape the bullets of white soldiers who were, in the phrasing of the time, not "discriminating" when they fired.

After this there are individual stories and individual perspectives, but no coherent narrative of the events at Sand Creek. The fighting, nearly every witness agreed, "became general." Companies pursued their own objectives with no knowledge of or concern for a governing strategy. Individual white men set out in pursuit of individual Indian people, and the struggles dispersed for miles up Sand Creek. Rather than one concerted charge met by one clear line of defense, the encounter became a free-for-all, with no center, no point of view from which the whole could be observed, and no central source of command. Whatever else Sand Creek was, it was a case study in the disintegration of leadership—of officers who did not control their men, officers who may well have thought that such control was beside the point. The men, after all, were doing what they had come to do: killing Indians.

But the troops were not killing Indians alone. When the Indians fled to the bed of Sand Creek, white soldiers took positions on opposite sides of the creek. Firing at the Indians in the center, the soldiers put each other at risk; some of the white casualties were caused by this "friendly fire." Colonel Chivington later reported that eight white men were killed, thirty-eight were wounded, and two later died of their wounds. With friendly fire from their own comrades, and with resistance from some Indian men trying to defend their people, white men at Sand Creek felt genuinely at risk. The troops saw acquaintances shot with arrows and bullets; they saw comrades dying. To some of the white participants, the engagement at Sand Creek *felt* like a battle, and not like a massacre, for the good reason that they were scared to death.

How many Indians were killed? Chivington and those who supported him insisted that they had fought hundreds of warriors and killed around five hundred Indian men. And yet, working from a total of around 130 lodges in the village with a usual population of five people to a lodge, there could not have been many more than five hundred to six hundred Indian people—children, women, and men—on the site. Contrary to Chivington's suggestion of five hundred dead warriors, most estimates range from 120 to 175 dead, with a frequent guess that over half were women and children.

Numbers, however, are a poor way to convey the reality of violence. Testimony given by contemporaries carries more force, but this is a kind of prose to which listeners and readers develop quick immunities. Using too many first-hand descriptions of the effects of violence is a sure way to put unintended distance between the event and the audience. Consider, then, only three passages from witnesses at Sand Creek, describing the condition of the dead Indians:

All manner of depredations were inflicted on their persons; they were scalped, their brains knocked out; the men used their knives, ripped open women,

clubbed little children, knocked them in the head with their guns, beat their brains out, mutilated their bodies in every sense of the word.[5]

In going over the battle-ground the next day, I did not see a body of man, woman, or child but was scalped, and in many instances their bodies were mutilated in the most horrible manner, men, women, and children—privates cut out, &c. I heard one man say that he had cut a woman's private parts out, and had them for exhibition on a stick; I heard another man say that he had cut the finger off of an Indian to get the rings on the hand. . . . I also heard of numerous instances in which men had cut out the private parts of females, and stretched them over the saddle-bow, and wore them over their hats, while riding in the ranks.[6]

Question: How many Indians were killed?
Answer: That I cannot say, as I did not go up above to count them. I only saw eight. I could not stand it; they were cut up too much.[7]

"I could not stand it; they were cut up too much": if I imagine an audience of tourists at Sand Creek looking at me as this last quotation hangs in the air, I do not know what to say next. I cannot find the point or the punch line. I can imagine my audience asking, "Why did you tell us this terrible story?" And to that, my only answer would be, "Because Drex Brooks thought that you should know."

A Twelve-Point Guide to War: Propositions to Have on One's Mind as One Looks at Drex Brooks's Photographs and Thinks About What Happened on These Sites

In graduate school, we were trained to be finders of themes. Where others might see a bunch of unconnected facts, we were obligated to locate the underlying patterns. Like any exercise, this was hard at first, but easier with practice. And, unlike many exercises, this one was addictive. In a world so overloaded with complexity and contradiction, the activity of getting a grip on themes and patterns can be genuinely comforting and soothing. This ability of generalizations to bring calm is particularly appealing when one confronts ugly forms of human behavior. In that spirit, I now present twelve patterns of white/Indian wars. These are not universal laws; readers will, no doubt, think of many exceptions as they read. But the most that one can ask of one's historical patterns is that they are true more often than are not, and these easily meet that qualification.

To give these general patterns a clear tie to reality, I have prefaced each point with a story from the Modoc War of 1872–73. I have chosen this war because it clearly and directly embodies most of these patterns, because it makes a geographical break from the usual Great Plains–centered tellings of the Indian wars, reminding us that these wars occurred all over the nation, and because it is a representatively agonizing war story.

Modoc Story, Part 1

The Modoc War began on November 29, 1872.[8] Interaction between whites and Modocs began long before that. In the 1820s, traders from the Hudson's Bay Company came into Modoc territory, at the border of what are now the states of California and Oregon. Like many tribes, the Modocs enthusiastically adopted European-introduced horses. In the late 1840s, white settlers in Oregon laid out wagon roads through Modoc territory, providing both a route to and from California and a more southern line of access from the Oregon Trail. These roads provided opportunities for raiding and killing, as the Modocs and other Indians of the area responded to the presence of white travelers with livestock and well-packed wagons. Both civilian vigilante groups and federal troops reacted to these attacks, sometimes "punishing" Indians who had taken part in the raiding and sometimes simply attacking any Indians they could find. Gold discoveries brought miners into the area, and ranchers and farmers also settled in. Newly founded towns were magnets for Indians as well as whites; Modocs were frequent visitors to the town of Yreka, with some Modoc women serving as prostitutes, and both women and men proving susceptible to the appeal of alcohol. Modocs worked, as well, as cowboys on some of the local ranches. By the time of the war in 1872, the denim and calico clothes worn by many Modocs were only one of the marks of change in their habits. In battles during the war, the men shouted insults at white troops, expertly wielding their familiarity with the English language to rile up the enemy.

Pattern 1:
Before a war happened, there was already
a great deal of water under the bridge.

Before whites and Indians would feel inclined to fight each other in a sustained way, they had to get to know each other. Before prolonged violence came disease, exotic plants and animals, traders and trade dependence, intermarriage, missionaries, representatives of the federal government, and, often enough, white emigrants, farmers, miners, or ranchers. Before they took up arms against each other, Indians and whites had to go through a substantial "getting to know you" phase. But, unlike the pattern in the musical *The King and I,* "getting to know you" in these situations often meant "getting to dislike and distrust you," "getting to realize that, even though I thought I could use your presence for my benefit, it is not working out that way."

The "getting to know you" phase was often so long and consequential that the border between "whites" and "Indians" became blurred. Intermarriage was the most obvious example of this blurring. Where traders had been present for a while, children of mixed heritage became important figures in society, sometimes caught uncomfortably between groups, sometimes finding their status-in-between

to be the source of considerable advantage. After a generation or two, the terms "Indian" and "white" had become more matters of political loyalty and cultural practice, than of lines of biological descent. Through intermarriage, natives and invaders had become, in the broadest sense, relatives; under those circumstances, Indian/white wars looked more like a quarrel between neighbors than a collision of strangers.

Interaction with whites, moreover, reshaped tribal economies and politics. Decades, sometimes centuries, of diplomacy, exchange, and negotiation preceded warfare, and Indian economies and forms of leadership showed the impact. Every time an Indian fired a gun in a battle, the use of a manufactured firearm offered another reminder of how intertwined the lives of the participants had already become.

Modoc Story, Part 2

In 1864, representatives of the federal government tried to negotiate an understanding with the Modocs and the other Indians of the area. But confusion was built into the process. In February of 1864, Elijah Steele, a judge and Indian agent for northern California, took part in discussions with the Modoc and two other tribes. By the terms of the Steele treaty, the Indians would cease to fight each other; they would not interfere with white settlers; although they would retain the right to travel, they would agree to be regulated by the officers at Fort Klamath. The Steele treaty did not address the question of whether the Modocs would have a reservation near the Lost River, their home area; it did not, by the same token, suggest that this was impossible. While the Steele treaty was at least moderately compatible with the Modocs' preference, it never received approval by the Indian Bureau or ratification by the United States Senate. Instead, in October of 1864, another negotiator—J. W. Pettit Huntington, superintendent of Indian affairs for Oregon—presided over a second set of discussions. The result was a second treaty (never ratified), setting forth very different terms, terms much less acceptable to the Modocs, since this treaty would send them away from Lost River.

The second treaty created one reservation for both the Klamath and the Modocs. This land that made up the reservation was entirely Klamath land; the Modocs would have to leave their homes and move into the homeland of another, sometimes hostile tribe. The Modocs divided over this prospect: some of them followed the leader Old Schonchin to the reservation and agreed to live there, despite frequent friction with the Klamath people. But another group left the reservation and returned to Lost River, repudiating the second treaty of 1864, while keeping their allegiance to the unratified Steele treaty. Kientpoos, or Captain Jack, emerged as the leader of this group.

White settlers in the Lost River country were not happy to see these original inhabitants return. Badgered by settlers' complaints of property damage and threats from the Modocs, federal officials suc-

ceeded in getting the Indians to return to the reservation—briefly. In the winter of 1869, A. B. Meacham, now the superintendent of Indian affairs for Oregon, persuaded Captain Jack and his fellows to go to the reservation. Then, in late April 1870, to the dismay of the settlers, Captain Jack's Modocs left the reservation and returned to Lost River. To Captain Jack and his party, the Steele treaty was the agreement with which they were still complying, and nothing in that treaty required them to live far from home in the company of the irritating Klamath. The treaty, the reservation, and all the various efforts to control the situation, launched by the officials of the United States Army and the Indian Bureau, had finally produced a perfect muddle.

Pattern 2:
Before a war occurred, some men representing the federal government declared that they were going to settle everything, and instead left everyone confused; that confusion was often the trigger for the war.

The Constitution declared the centrality of federal responsibility in Indian affairs, giving Congress the power "to regulate commerce with foreign nations, among the several states, and with the Indian tribes." Thus there was a constitutionally based reason for federal officials to swing into action in anticipation of conflict and to try to arrange a peace that would serve two not-very-compatible goals: the expansion of white commerce and settlement, and the preservation and assimilation of the Indians.

And so a phalanx of territorial politicians, Indian agents, military officers, and humanitarians and reformers called for and attended hundreds of meetings with Indian people. At those meetings, the white officials declared their good intentions and their hopes for harmony between whites and Indians. While some of them were cheerful liars, veiling land grabs under the rhetoric of paternalistic helpfulness, many others believed the things they said.

Frequently the outcome of these councils and negotiations hinged on the honesty and efficiency of one person: the interpreter, who had to translate not only two very different languages, but also two very different systems of property and law. Opportunities for confusion were unlimited. Merely identifying who, on either the tribal or federal side, had the authority to ratify and to enforce an agreement could be the most difficult part of these negotiations. White officials fell into the habit of selecting and identifying certain leaders as "chiefs," and then declaring that a whole tribe had agreed to cede territory and retreat to a reservation, when, in fact, only a few, not-always-respected individuals from the tribe had signed an agreement.

From these federal efforts to anticipate conflict and reach a resolution came agreements that carried very different meanings to different individuals and groups. With their multiple meanings, the agreements were very difficult to enforce. On the federal side, a breakdown of enforcement was built into a policy stretched to the point of snapping, with an official goal of benevolence to Indians pulling in one direction, and an insistent white demand for lands and resources pulling in another.

Federal officials had visions of sharing the benefits of civilization and Christianity with grateful Indians; Indians had visions of maintaining their sovereignty and traditional economies; white settlers had visions of owning and using land without Indian interference. The federal negotiators and commissioners were placed exactly at the point where those visions clashed. It was not, therefore, unusual to find federal commissioners playing the part of the recipients of everyone's wrath, as both Indians and whites cast these negotiators as the bumblers whose negotiations had delivered everyone into confusion and conflict.

The effectiveness of federal intervention was undermined, as well, by the weakness of the government's power through the first century of the nation's existence. American citizens had a principled distrust of an established, well-funded army. Monarchies and tyrannies relied on standing armies. But democracies and republics called up citizen militias to deal with emergencies and then disbanded those militias when the emergencies were resolved. Here, then, was a curious reluctance to face up to the fact that the nation was engaged, not in occasional military emergencies, but in a prolonged and concerted war for the continent, a war that would not be won without a serious army, seriously funded. The ideology of expansion may have offered an image of inferior Indians who would simply melt away as white settlements expanded, but few tribes chose to melt and many chose to fight. The cost of war weighed on the federal treasury, principled opposition to a standing army or not. At the end of a war, the supporters of thrift would reappear, cutting back the army's funding and size, and leaving the federal government in a chronic position of weakness when it came to enforcing its laws and standing by its promises.

Expenses aside, it was an awkward matter to use the United States Army against United States citizens. Even though the army did sometimes try to remove white squatters and intruders from Indian territory, this was hardly the way to make the army more popular. Unable to deliver on many of its promises and guarantees, the federal effort to get the jump on conflict and to negotiate peaceful agreements frequently added up to the achievement of giving all the partisans someone to blame when those agreements fell apart.

Modoc Story, Part 3

In November of 1872, the pieces and parts of the federal government geared up for action. Replacing A. B. Meacham, and too recently arrived in his job to know much about the Modocs, Thomas B. Odeneal, the new superintendent of Indian affairs for Oregon, asked Major John T. Green to send troops from Fort Klamath, to arrest Captain Jack and return him and his people to the Klamath Reservation. Selected by Green, Major James Jackson and thirty-eight soldiers took a long, miserable ride through rain and sleet. Several armed civilians joined in the enterprise. On the early morning of November 29, 1872, the Lost River Modocs were camped in two sites. The army prepared to enter the larger of the two camps, the one with Captain Jack in it, while the civilians took on the smaller camp. Jackson and his men proposed to disarm the Modocs; the Modocs held on to their guns and rifles. In this tense situation, shooting suddenly started. Finding that they were in way over their heads, the civilians retreated—fast—from the smaller camp. The regular troops held on to the larger camp, but the Modocs fled and the troops did not pursue them. After burning the village, with Captain Jack now far beyond the reach of the army, Captain Jackson led a retreat of his own to a neighboring ranch.

While most of the Modocs headed off to take refuge in the nearby Lava Beds, a small group of men rode off to vent their anger on the nearby settlers. In his retreat, Captain Jackson had not tried to warn settlers in the area, much less to offer them protection. A group including Hooker Jim, Boston Charley, Long Tim, and others—*but not Captain Jack*—stopped at several neighboring ranches, killing men and male children, but sparing women. At their first stop, Hooker Jim and his allies killed a settler named William Boddy, along with Boddy's son-in-law, Nicholas Schira. Abruptly and terribly widowed, Mrs. Boddy and Mrs. Schira hid during the night and fled to refuge the next morning, while the Modoc party went on to attack other whites, killing fourteen altogether.

The bungled attempt to arrest Captain Jack triggered the war. The vengeance imposed by a few Modocs on the unwarned and unprepared white settlers made the momentum for war irreversible.

Pattern 3:
The first acts of violence usually were more
accidents of impulse and passion than the
considered and chosen opening acts
of an intended war.

At the end of a war, it was common for leaders—both white and Indian—to offer some version of this sentiment: "We did not want this war; it happened in spite of us." When they said this, they were not lying. On the contrary, they were recording the fact that at the start of the war, the preferences of the leaders did not carry nearly as much weight as the impatience and anger of a few individuals. On the Indian side, the first acts of violence were often committed by impulsive young men, driven by their ambition as warriors and defiant of the restraints imposed by their elders. Hunger was also a common provocation for violence. In the gritty details of daily life, invasion and conquest meant, at the bedrock, a loss of traditional sources of food for Indians, and

there are few better triggers for desperate acts than the prospect of starvation. On the white side, the triggering acts of violence often came from a similar impatience in white settlers who felt that the United States Army was far too slow in coming to their aid and who therefore took it upon themselves to "punish" Indians for various "crimes," especially for theft. These acts of retaliation were often committed in defiance of white officials, who had a better grasp on the proposition that white American notions of "crime" and "punishment" made an uneven fit to the complex reality of incompatible groups with conflicting ambitions trying to live as neighbors.

Individualistic in their origins, these opening episodes of violence placed leaders in positions where their range of choice was much diminished. Repeatedly, the heated acts of a few individuals carried more weight than the restraint and caution which leaders had tried to maintain. Here came the turning point in the escalation of violence: white settlers and officials chose to take the acts of a few impatient Indian people to represent the will of the whole group. With that assumption embraced, everyone—women, children, and men who had not picked a fight—had to be punished for the actions of a few. Once that choice was made, the unrolling of the war might have seemed inevitable. But it is crucial to remember that there were *two* paths leading from this fork in the road, and neither was inevitable. Humans, in circumstances like these, have the capacity to distinguish individual actions from group actions and to calibrate their responses with that distinction in mind. Here is the clearest contribution of hindsight: if that capacity to make distinctions had been more often in play, the mortality and misery rate in these wars would have been much diminished.

Modoc Story, Part 4

When Hooker Jim's party, reacting to the soldiers' attack on their camp, killed some of their white neighbors, panicked rumors spread in all directions. In towns and in ranch houses, settlers panicked, anticipating brutal surprises from all directions. From the security of hindsight, it is clear that whites who settled in Modoc territory had been taking a great risk, insisting on their right to live in contested terrain. But the killings committed by Hooker Jim's party cast the whites as undeserving victims, delivered by their innocence and trust to the knives and bullets of treacherous Indians. For most settlers in the area, the Lost River killings settled the question. *All* the nonreservation Modocs had to be punished, and what hindsight would call a war of conquest or displacement proved, at the time, to be a conflict in which the whites felt that *they* were the ones who had been mistreated and who were fully justified in defending themselves before the next outrage could occur.

Pattern 4:
If Indians tried to terrorize settlers into leaving contested territory, whites instantly saw themselves as the innocent victims and Indians as the guilty aggressors, and thus the question of justification seemed settled.

Throughout history, humans have found various ways to communicate the message, "Get out; we don't want you here." Snubbing, shunning, segregation, economic boycotts, eviction notices, elimination of a food supply, threats, property destruction, torture, and murder: all of these gestures have been used to say to their recipients, "We'd just as soon you got out of here." When whites moved into territory that Indians claimed, and especially, when white settlement interfered with Indian food-growing and food-gathering, Indians turned to these various devices of communication to say, effectively and memorably, "Get out."

At various places and times, delivering this message to white intruders, Indian people used the full vocabulary of terror: fire, kidnapping, rape, murder, and mutilation. Because of the brutality practiced in these episodes, moral judgment of the Indian wars will never be pure or clear. Rather than trying to be saints of nonviolence and passive resistance, Indians could be cruel and arbitrary in their attacks on white families whose ambitions had led them to the wrong place at the wrong time.

Contemplating these attacks, historians become "equal opportunity cynics," seeing neither nobility nor brutality as the exclusive property of any group. While Indian attacks on white families have mixed and blurred the moral vision of historians, they sharpened and clarified the moral judgments of white settlers and officials. Once the Indians tried to terrorize settlers into leaving, in the minds of Anglo-Americans, the roles of aggressor and victim instantly reversed. Whites ceased to register as invaders and provokers of conflict, and occupied, instead, the status of innocent victims. With this shift, the question of justification was settled: Indians had started the trouble and had asked for punishment, and whites could do whatever they had to do, in order to defend themselves.

Modoc Story, Part 5

After the violence at Lost River, the Modocs crossed Tule Lake and took refuge in an extraordinary place, the Lava Beds of northern California. When he heard the news of the bungled arrest and the flight of the Modocs, Lieutenant Colonel Frank Wheaton, Green's and Jackson's commanding officer, felt considerable confidence in his understanding of what to do next. He would assemble a force composed of units of both Regulars and California and Oregon volunteers, and he would march into the Lava Beds toward the Modoc Stronghold in the center, encircle the renegades, and defeat them. "I do not believe we need anticipate a continued resistance from this little band of Modocs," Wheaton told General E. R. S. Canby.[9] Canby, in turn, reported cheerfully: "I do not think the operations will be protracted."[10] In Washington, General William Tecumseh Sherman synthesized the various messages of confidence he had received from the West Coast, and told the secretary of war that Canby "is in actual command of all the troops and resources of the country and will doubtless bring this matter to a satisfactory end."[11]

On January 17, 1873, Lieutenant Colonel Wheaton tried to put this confident plan into action. But a clumsy troop movement the night before had alerted the Modocs and sacrificed the advantage of surprise. In the morning, a dense fog covered the ground. The troops started forward and presented themselves as targets for Modoc bullets, often expertly delivered. The soldiers could see the injuries and deaths produced by these bullets, but with the thick fog and the rocky, ridge-broken landscape, they could seldom see the Indians who were firing on them. Demoralized, the troops ground to a halt; officers could not or would not follow the original plan to encircle the Stronghold. By nightfall, the United States forces were in a disorderly retreat, leaving behind, for the Modocs' use, many of their firearms and much of their ammunition, and abandoning many of the wounded. The January 17 attack proved to be a complete disaster for the whites, with the advantage shifting to the Modocs, who did not lose one warrior. Fewer than sixty Modoc men had defeated three hundred soldiers.

Pattern 5:
The wars often began with an Indian victory, frequently because whites were over-confident and

thought that fighting a primitive, unsophisticated enemy would be easy and quick.

By all the tenets of white American pride, it should have been easy to beat a set of disorderly, undisciplined primitives. That excess of confidence, however, often led to an initial defeat, as white troops plunged into battle confidently, certain that they had a clear advantage over a simple foe. A belief in one's own intrinsic superiority, these early battles demonstrated, could be a dangerous, even lethal delusion. The defeats put American forces through a rough period of reassessment, leading to the necessary recognition that Indian war was serious business, requiring serious commitments of leadership, discipline, equipment, and, especially, funding. The defeats reinforced, moreover, the vision of the whites as the embattled, besieged victims, further obscuring the bedrock reality of white invasion, encroachment, and aggression. Perhaps most important, these losses made whites furious, determined on vengeance and unwilling to consider alternatives to the escalation of the war.

Modoc Story, Part 6

During the war, a significant number of Modocs stayed on the Klamath Reservation, with some sympathetic, some simply neutral, and some opposed to Captain Jack and his group. While the army decided not to try to use Modocs against Modocs, some Klam-

ath Indians took part in the January 17 attack on the Lava Beds. When the battle turned against the army, officers placed some of the blame on the Klamaths for fighting half-heartedly. The army then recruited a number of Indian auxiliaries from the Warm Springs Reservation. These Indians found cooperation with whites to be, on occasion, a life-threatening challenge. On one occasion, late in the war, the Warm Springs Indians tried to come to the aid of a group of soldiers who had been ambushed by Modocs. Panicked and unthinking, the soldiers fired on their rescuers. Despite every effort on the part of the Warm Springs Indians to identify themselves as friends, they could not get their "allies" to stop shooting at them.

By the end of the war, any notions of tribal solidarity had been shattered. Captain Jack had never been an enthusiastic advocate of war. The impulsive acts of Hooker Jim's party, in killing the Lost River settlers, had forced Captain Jack into a war he did not want. In the spring of 1873, as federal officials tried for a negotiated resolution to the war, the Modoc militants pressured Jack into taking part in a treacherous attack on the peace commissioners. On April 11, 1873, the Modocs killed Reverend Eleazar Thomas and General E. R. S. Canby (the only general killed in the Indian wars) and seriously wounded Albert Meacham. In May of 1873, Hooker Jim, Steamboat Frank, Shacknasty Jim, and Bogus Charley, members of the war party, left Captain Jack and surrendered to the Americans. Over the next weeks, the Modoc men who had pushed Captain Jack into war and assassination now served as his betrayers, helping the army track him down for a final capture.

In July of 1873, Captain Jack and five others were tried and convicted for the murder of the commissioners. Hooker Jim, and others of the original war advocates, were not tried for either the murder of the Lost River settlers or the killings of the commissioners. On the contrary, the army rewarded them for their betrayal of Captain Jack by exempting them from punishment, in order to set an example that would encourage other Indians to change sides. Captain Jack was obviously very much troubled by this chain of betrayal. "I didn't know anything of any settlers being killed until Hooker Jim came with his band and told me," he said at his trial. None of his own people "had killed any of the whites, and I had never told Hooker Jim and his party to murder any settlers; and I did not want them to stay with me." Hooker Jim was "the one that always wanted to fight, and commenced killing and murdering." But now, Captain Jack said, "I have to bear the blame for him and the rest of them."[12]

Pattern 6:
The idea of an "Indian war" as a conflict of whites against Indians seldom had much to do with reality because Indians were usually on both sides of the conflict.

Intertribal conflict began long before the arrival of Europeans or Euro-Americans. In some areas, the introduction of horses and guns increased the stakes and intensity of intertribal raiding and war. All over North America, the expansion of white settlement escalated the conflict among tribes, as they struggled for control of a reduced supply of territory and resources. Under those circumstances, it made perfect sense for members of one tribe to see whites as helpful allies in campaigns against the common enemy of another tribe. It made sense, as well, to exercise a warrior's skills and take advantage of the opportunity presented by the army's need for scouts and auxiliaries who knew the terrain and the ways of the enemy.

Divisions in war came, as well, from the presence of factions within tribes. The boundaries of identity and loyalty to a particular tribe were flexible; the band, or the clan, or the family was more likely to be the primary unit of social cohesion. Conquest placed, moreover, a terrible strain on leadership. To some leaders, going along with whites and their treaties and reservations seemed like the wisest response to an unhappy situation; to leaders of a different persuasion, resistance—armed, if necessary—seemed the best way to serve their people's interests. In some cases, missionaries had split the tribe between those who had converted to Christianity, and those who held to the traditional beliefs and practices. And, true to human nature, conflicts of personality and of individual ambition played their role in dividing tribes.

Facing up to the divisions inside and among Indian

groups requires one to pay attention to one's own un-examined sentimentality. Many late-twentieth-century Americans, of all ethnicities, remain susceptible to a romantic wish that the victims of white American aggression had stood together, measuring up to a standard for saintly, noble, heroic solidarity that any human population, living in perfectly happy and tranquil times, would have had a hard time meeting. But put humans under the terrible pressure of conquest, and the record discloses the great muddle that is human nature.

Modoc Story, Part 7

In the course of the Modoc War, the whites did not do much better than the Indians at maintaining solidarity. Blaming each other took nearly as much of their time and energy as did fighting Modocs. Before the war began, some federal officials put considerable effort into arguing that the whole situation had been produced by the actions of "bad" whites, who had given the Modocs bad advice and encouraged them in their resistance. When the plan to arrest Jack exploded into war, some whites blamed Superintendent Odeneal for acting in ill-considered haste (and for keeping himself at a safe distance from the scene of danger). Some blamed Captain Jackson for letting the arrest action get out of control, for refusing to pursue the Modocs, and for failing to warn the neighboring settlers of their danger.

After the January 17 defeat of the army, blamers and faultfinders launched into a second round of activity. After that debacle, Wheaton was replaced by Colonel Alvan C. Gillem. Not a particularly charismatic fellow, troubled by ill health, Gillem gained a reputation for reluctance to take on the Modocs, and evoked considerable hostility from his officers. For the rest of the war, divisions ran in all directions: officers of the army against representatives of the Indian Office; Regulars against volunteers; the governor of Oregon against the appointed officials of the federal government; Oregonians against Californians (judged by the Oregonians to be too sympathetic to the Modocs); officers against local merchants and farmers who sold the army provisions and supplies for a handsome profit; eastern humanitarians standing up for the Modocs' rights against both the army and the settlers. The effort to form the Modoc Peace Commission was itself a fine demonstration of the disunity of whites. When A. B. Meacham was asked to serve with his successor as superintendent of Indian affairs in Oregon, Thomas Odeneal, Meacham, who felt Odeneal was responsible for the whole mess, held up the process until a commissioner more agreeable to Meacham could replace Odeneal. Long before they tried to negotiate with the Modocs, the Peace Commission had a hard enough time simply finding personnel who could peaceably talk with each other.

The Modoc War's most distressing examples of the breakdown of white solidarity came in a few episodes in which uninjured soldiers refused to help the wounded during retreats. During the retreat from the January 17 defeat, the soldiers scrambled up a bluff to safety: "No one," Keith Murray notes, "helped anyone else, and the walking wounded were left to climb the hill as best they could." After another army defeat, lost at night, the soldiers who could still walk "tried to avoid helping to carry the stretchers" of the wounded.[13] White Americans did not march, in unity and harmony, to the conquest of the continent. White Americans did not retreat in any better order.

Pattern 7:
Whites were often quite disunited themselves, so disunited that white Americans sometimes looked as if they might kill each other before the Indians got a chance at them.

The impact of Indian war on white society resembled the impact of a rock on a window, a window that does not shatter entirely but still shows cracks that spread in all directions. The fractures ran right through the center of the federal government; the Office of Indian Affairs and the War Department were jealous of each other's turf, and often opposed in their policies. The president frequently received conflicting advice from the various officials working in Indian affairs; these were not the circumstances to give rise to a coherent and consistent federal policy. In some cases, the lack of coordination and communication between Indian agents and army officers was, directly and concretely, the cause of war.

The army on its own was a fissured society. Personal rivalry and conflicting ambitions divided the officers. Personality conflicts were often heightened by the conditions of isolation and remoteness; it is not too much to say that some of these men truly hated each other. Young officers were often impatient with the restraints imposed by older officers; especially after the Civil War, as opportunities for promotion narrowed, a sense of frustrated ambition spread through the officer corps. Some of the most heated conflicts centered on supplies, as officers out on the front lines struggled with inadequate food, firearms, clothing, and transportation. Enlisted men, in the meantime, felt varying degrees of enthusiasm and loyalty for their officers and for the whole cause and campaign in which they were employed. Sometimes the soldiers experienced true crises of confidence, convinced that they were trusting their lives to leaders without wisdom or sense. The most unmistakable expression of discontent and demoralization came in the fact of a high rate of desertion.

The greatest division in the fighting force was the gap between Regulars and volunteers. Local citizens who joined militia units or who simply rode along as informal volunteers often saw the army as plodding, cautious, and too easy on the Indians. Raids, retaliations, and acts of terror had built up strong currents of racial hostility; local volunteers often wanted to hit the Indians hard, fast, and indiscriminately. On the other hand, volunteers stood a good chance of being undrilled and undisciplined, susceptible to panic and flight at the most crucial moments. On a number of occasions, when volunteers complained about Regulars and Regulars complained about volunteers, in this tense and angry relationship between two elements of the white American population, there seemed to be little room left over for any attention to the Indian enemy.

Another important element of white disunity appeared in the dissenters, whites who for various reasons disapproved of the course of action taken by the army. Sometimes these were settlers who had gotten to know Indians under tranquil and collaborative circumstances. Men and women like these sympathized with the misfortunes of their Indian neighbors, tried to help them secure permanent land claims, and complained of the Army's inflexibility and harshness. Another group of dissenters wore Army uniforms. It was not uncommon, after a massacre or vicious battle, to find a few soldiers or officers who were repelled by what they had seen or taken part in. In some cases, officers felt that their own honor had been violated; they had taken a group of Indians to be peaceful, had promised them safety, and then been unable to protect them from attack. These officers were surprisingly outspoken in expressing their dissent. But the loudest of objections came from men and women far from the battlefield—humanitarians who registered their dismay and disapproval when they looked at the actions of the army and hostile western settlers. After the Civil War, these humanitarians coalesced as a significant lobby with real power. Army officers thus spent part of their time anticipating criticisms and denunciations from the humanitarians. These agents of "Manifest Destiny" could feel themselves to be besieged on all sides: constantly challenged and often outfoxed by the Indians, denounced by the eastern humanitarians for their cruelty, and damned by western settlers for their unwillingness to punish the Indians with proper harshness.

From time to time, the United States government has been denounced for its "genocidal" policies against Indians. But once you have examined the intensity and range of division within the white population, and even within the forces officially detailed to Indian affairs, then there is one clear defense against the accusations of genocide: even though some individuals did call for the extermination of the Indians, white Americans were simply too divided and disorganized to implement such a policy, even if a majority had supported it.

Modoc Story, Part 8

The Modoc people knew the landscape of the Lava Beds, and the whites did not. The Lava Beds provided the Indians with pockets of water and ice, with places to hide cattle, and with caves that could withstand bombardment. The landscape was shaped by parallel ridges of rocks which worked perfectly to the Modocs' advantage. The rock ridges were natural fortifications; the passages between the ridges served as corridors and pathways that permitted the Modocs to keep shifting their sparse number of warriors to new and unexpected locations. On January 17, 1873, as the Regulars and the volunteers sat miserably in the mist and absorbed bullets that seemed to have been fired by the fog itself, the Indians' advantage in knowing the turf was the most compelling reality that the soldiers had to contemplate.

On April 26, 1873, a party of soldiers under Captain Evan Thomas went to the Lava Beds on a reconnaissance. In the early afternoon, the party sat down for an unguarded lunch. The Modoc ambush that came down upon them caught them completely by surprise. Many of the soldiers died on the spot; many more *would* have died if the Indians had not stopped the attack, when the Modoc leader Scarfaced Charley called out, "All you fellows that ain't dead had better go home. We don't want to kill you all in one day." Twenty-three of the Americans were killed, and nineteen wounded. Thomas's force, in historian Keith Murray's words, "had lost almost as many men in two hours as the entire army had lost thus far in the war." Just as they had during the January 17 battle, the Modocs "suffered no losses."[14]

The moment of the Modocs' ceasefire was by no means the end of the surviving soldiers' distress. Still to be reckoned with was the landscape. The relief party coming to their aid got lost. The doctor, traveling behind the relief party, also got lost. Walk-ing the next night in a storm, carrying the wounded, the relief party tried to follow "guides" who "had no idea where they were going," putting the wounded through an awful, aimless ordeal of jostling and bumping against rocks. Knowing where you were, how to get out of there, and how to get to where you would rather be added up to a large element of success and survival in this campaign, and this was an element very much balanced toward the Modocs. "We seem," one of the army's high-ranking officers telegraphed after the Thomas incident, "to be acting somewhat in the dark."[15]

Pattern 8:
The fact that the Indians knew the landscape, terrain, food supply, and water sources put the whites at a considerable disadvantage.

A century after the Indian wars, "the lessons of Vietnam" became a commonly used phrase. The lessons of Vietnam hinged on the maddening realities of fighting a guerrilla war. The more confident Americans were of their technological superiority and greater wealth, the more vulnerable they were to an enemy who relied on other strengths entirely. In the jungles of Southeast Asia, Americans finally had to recognize the crippling disadvantages of being the intruders and strangers, trying to impose their will in a terrain the natives knew far better.

And yet it is no easy matter to distinguish "the lessons of the Indian wars" from "the lessons of

Vietnam." In the territory that would become the United States, the natives knew the terrain, the travel routes, the easily defensible locations, the climate, the location of water, and the sources of food. Their knowledge formed a great contrast with the ignorance, on all these topics, of most army officers and soldiers. The Indian population could, moreover, shift back and forth between hostile and friendly, enemy and ally, in a way that left whites puzzled, jumpy, and frustrated. In the space of a few hours, a warrior raiding a settlement or fighting hard against the army could become a family man, relaxed and at peace in his village.

Whatever whites may have thought about the superiority of their technology or their civilization, those assumptions of superiority did not do them much good on the battlefield. If anything, their excess of confidence played into the hands of the enemy. When full of confidence, whites were set up to fall for decoys and predisposed to cooperate with ambushes. Imagining the course of the war, far from the actual battlefield, officers could convince themselves of the effectiveness of their own grand plans and strategies, and then watch those visions dissolve under the pressure of difficult and disorienting terrain, impossible supply lines, and an enemy who simply knew more than they did about the place of contest.

The lessons of the Indian/white wars and the lessons of the Vietnam war were striking similar, for the obvious reason that they were both the lessons of guerrilla war, the kind of war in which the local, insider knowledge held by the natives gave them a great advantage. The invaders, by contrast, were decidedly out of their place. They had to work with the constant burden of over-stretched and over-strained chains of communication and supply. At the most awkward moments, the invaders simply lost their bearings. Contemplating the Indian/white wars, one cannot avoid the conclusion that much of what we have taken to thinking of as "the lessons of Vietnam" was available for learning a century or more ago.

Modoc Story, Part 9

When the Modoc men fled Lost River for the Lava Beds, there was never a question of dividing families. Women and children went with the men; women and children occupied the Stronghold along with the warriors; women and children, despite the close presence of soldiers, escaped from the Stronghold with the warriors in April of 1873. There were no exemptions on the basis of gender or age from the migrations and hardships of this war.

For the first rounds of the war, the army's inability to close with the Modocs limited any opportunity for injuring or killing noncombatants. On April 16, 1873, when the Modocs left the Stronghold and the army occupied it, hostility toward noncombatants boiled to the surface. Three old Modoc men were found alive in the Stronghold, and one woman.

Two of the men and the woman "were shot by soldiers," Modoc War historian Richard Dillon reports. "The third man was stoned to death by the Warm Springs" Indians. White soldiers "kicked the severed head of a Modoc like a soccer ball." Trooper Maurice Fitzgerald reported that he saw an aged "woman begging piteously for her life. 'Me no hurt no one, me no fight,' she whined." According to Fitzgerald's report, an officer then said, "'Is there anyone here who will put that old hag out of the way?' A Pennsylvania Dutchman stepped forward and said, 'I'll fix her, lieutenant.' He put the muzzle of his carbine to her head and blew it to pieces." Here, again, one has a hard time distinguishing "the lessons of the Indian wars" from "the lessons of Vietnam."[16]

After Hooker Jim's party had killed the Lost River settlers at the start of the war, civilians in southern Oregon were wild for revenge. At the end of the war, one party of Modocs surrendered to a white man, John Fairchild, who had tried to be a peacemaker. John Fairchild's brother James started off with the captives in a wagon to take them to the army. Two white men stopped the wagon, forced Fairchild away, and "fired into the wagon at almost point-blank range," killed four men, and wounded one woman.[17] In circumstances like these, individual guilt or innocence could not be the determinant of one's fate; being Modoc and falling into the hands of vindictive whites were the two key components of a death sentence.

People writing with disapproval about violence toward noncombatants in wartime can, intentionally or not, come close to trivializing or dismissing the terrible effects of violence on actual combatants. It is, therefore, important to take a moment to remember what it might mean to be injured in legitimate, certified combat. This is a description of the ordeal of Jerry Crooks, a member of the California Volunteers, during the retreat from the January 17 defeat:

> He had taken a rifle ball in one leg, which broke the bone so badly he could not be carried in a blanket. So he rode a pony with his leg dangling loosely. When it struck boulders or even stubborn sagebrush, the pain was terrible. Finally, his comrades tied a rope around the leg so that it could be lifted when his mount came to an obstacle. Still, [a companion] wrote, "It was sickening to see the expression on his face, and the pain he must have endured was excruciating."[18]

Pattern 9:
While some warriors and soldiers tried to keep a clear line between combatants and noncombatants, those efforts often broke down, in part because of confusion and in part because of pure hatred.

The conditions of guerrilla war carried their own grim logic. The invaders foundered in making distinctions—hostile from friendly, guilty from innocent, combatant from noncombatant. Demoralized and disoriented troops were men charged and ready for scapegoating, and not much interested in distinguishing between warriors and nonwarriors, men and women, adults and children. Moreover, Indian warriors were most often living in the midst of their families—because protecting the women and children was one of the principal obligations of the warriors, and because the wars were taking place in their homelands, in the areas where these families lived. If the army tried to make a surprise attack on the warriors, striking at dawn, women and children would be among the ones surprised. To the army, fighting Indians who were often nomadic, the greatest challenge lay in locating them. Give them advance warning, try to separate the combatants from the noncombatants, and you could lose all the advantages of surprise; you could, for that matter, lose your entire opportunity to attack. Given the greater knowledge the natives had of the terrain, it might well be a long time before that opportunity arose again.

These reasons, in part, explain the violence inflicted on noncombatants. Beyond reason, however, lies passion—an intensity of hatred and an embrace of brutality that could make a man see a child or an infant as an appropriate target for murder. For many historians, writing of these wars, it has been tempting to avoid these troubling issues, by taking the position that we cannot permit ourselves any moral or emotional responses to these events, because we cannot judge the events of the past by the standards of today. By this line of thought, the people who enthusiastically killed Indian women, children, and noncomba-

tant men were simply "men of their times," who operated under the standard attitudes and values of those times—attitudes and values that we, as creatures of another century, have no right to judge. But this argument is, finally, both inaccurate and dangerous.

It is inaccurate, because white American men of the nineteenth century had a wide range of attitudes and values, and we do them a considerable disservice when we write about them as if they had all submitted to the same, "Manifest Destiny," attitudinal cookie-cutter. Before adopting the "men of their times" model of moral homogeneity, one has an obligation to consider this haunting episode from the Bear River Massacre in 1863. Following the commands of his grandmother, the twelve-year-old Shoshone boy Yeager Timbimboo spent most of the day lying on the snow-covered ground, pretending to be dead. But at a crucial moment, he disobeyed his grandmother, and opened his eyes.

> A soldier came upon him and saw that he was alive and looking around. The military man stood over Yeager, his gun pointing at the young boy's head ready to fire. The soldier stared at the boy and the boy at the soldier. The second time the soldier raised his rifle the little boy knew his time to die was near. The soldier then lowered his gun and a moment later raised it again. For some reason he could not complete his task. He took his rifle down and walked away.[19]

"What went through this soldier's mind will never be known," said the Shoshone woman who told this story, but what went through this man's mind must be respected. It would be dangerous and chilling to say that we dare not use our own standards to respond to this man's moment of restraint and to find it heartening and impressive. If an ideal of historical detachment and objectivity requires us to hold to a scrupulous neutrality on the question of whether or not soldiers should shoot young children, then this is a professional ideal that corrodes the humanity of the historian.

The judgment of violence toward noncombatants is not, in any case, a matter of nineteenth-century standards in opposition to twentieth-century standards. It is just as much a matter of differences and conflicts among nineteenth-century white Americans themselves. In a number of the most violent episodes in this history, individual white officers and soldiers spoke out vigorously in opposition to what the majority had done. White officers opposed John Chivington's plan to attack at Sand Creek the day *before* the event; in the days and weeks after the massacre, some men in the army and some civilians continued to speak out against Chivington and his supporters. In 1871, a Tucson citizen named William Oury led a massacre of Apache families at Camp Grant, Arizona. Royal Whitman, the officer at Camp Grant who had promised the families a sanctuary, instantly and persistently protested the attack. Twentieth-century Americans owe Royal Whitman the recognition that he was not a creation of twentieth-century moral hindsight. Royal Whitman, denouncer

of the Camp Grant Massacre, was just as much a nineteenth-century man as William Oury, leader of the attack.

Modoc Story, Part 10

Captain Jack was a war leader who had not wanted war. He was, moreover, a leader with very limited power to impose his preferences on his people. On the contrary, he was often outmaneuvered by the war enthusiasts, pressured either to join them or admit to cowardice. Thus, even when the war had turned into a losing proposition, Captain Jack found it virtually impossible to persuade his people to reach a consensus for surrender. But Captain Jack confronted a relatively unusual situation in Indian war: a disposition, on the part of the federal government and its immediate representatives, to receive peace initiatives with some eagerness.

The result of these conditions was a pattern no doubt maddening to everyone involved: frequent indications, delivered through a variety of emissaries, that Captain Jack would like to surrender; optimism, on the part of some officials, that this might prove to be a route away from further carnage; and then a retreat on Jack's part, with the declaration that he could not surrender if it would mean that his people would have to leave Oregon, or that some would be tried and executed for the killings of settlers or commissioners. Two propositions were clear, and impossible to reconcile: Jack wanted out of the war, and yet he could find no way out.

Pattern 10:
It was no easy matter to surrender; getting out of a war was a lot harder than getting one started.

When Indians decided they had had enough of a war, whites were often reluctant to receive that message. These are agonizing events to contemplate; in the Black Hawk War in 1832, to use one conspicuous example, the Sauk leader Black Hawk tried three times to tell the American troops that he wanted this struggle to end, and each time, he was rebuffed and his people were attacked again. Reaching the decision to surrender was by no means an easy one for an Indian leader, but getting the whites to agree to recognize that decision could often prove even tougher.

Why this reluctance to take white flags seriously? Differences of language and custom made it difficult to communicate clearly any message at all, whether of belligerence or of peace. Suspicions of treachery preoccupied both sides; a white flag could be, and sometimes was, a trick, a way of getting the opponent to drop his guard before a duplicitous attack. Perhaps more important, after investing many lives and much money in a war, whites wanted to get the most out of that investment. They wanted the enemy pushed to the margin, forced to make an unconditional surrender and to accept whatever terms the winners wished to impose. The clearest way to make certain that a group would never fight again was to reduce them, materially and psychologically, past the prospect of recovery. And, perhaps most important, a spirit of revenge and retaliation so powered white actions that the implied response to surrender was this: "You want to make peace *now*, but it is too late; you should have thought of this before you started fighting."

Modoc Story, Part 11

In July of 1873, after some debates over the legality of a trial, a military hearing took place, with Captain Jack and five other Modoc men accused of murdering the peace commissioners in violation of a truce. The transcript of the hearing makes for painful reading. The presiding officer seemed willing to give the Modocs a chance to present their story, and an interpreter attended to translate for the accused. But the interpreter was also a witness for the prosecution; the Modocs had no attorney to represent them; and the whole procedure was clearly a foreign and discouraging process for them.

Early in the hearing, the transcript records this exchange: "The prisoners were then severally asked by the judge-advocate if they desired to introduce counsel; to which they severally replied in the negative; and that they had been unable to procure any." After each witness's testimony appears this notation: "The judge-advocate then asked the prisoners severally if they desired to cross-examine the witness, to which they replied in the negative." The feelings of men awaiting a life-or-death judgment from a process that was out of their control come through most strongly in Captain Jack's interruption in his address to the court. Speaking through an interpreter, Jack suddenly made this remark: "I hardly know how to talk here. I don't know how white people talk in such a place as this but I will do the best I can."[20]

Kept in a guardhouse at Fort Klamath after their conviction, Jack and his five comrades were taken out for hanging on October 3, 1873. When he was asked, the day before, if he had a last request, Captain Jack said, "I should like to live until I die a natural death."[21] Two of the younger Modocs had had their sentences commuted from death to life terms in Alcatraz, but the army had adopted the curious custom of refusing to reveal this clemency until the moment of execution. All the Modocs were required to watch as Captain Jack, Boston Charley, Schonchin Jim, and Black Jim were hanged. That night, someone removed Captain Jack's body from its grave.

The rest of the nonreservation Modocs—thirty-nine men, fifty-four women, and sixty children—were put on a train, with their destination concealed from them. They were temporarily placed at Fort McPherson, Nebraska, then moved to Baxter Springs, Kansas, and then finally permitted to resettle in Seneca Springs, at the Quapaw Agency in Indian Territory (present-day Oklahoma). In 1909, thirty-six years after their defeat, the Modocs who so chose were permitted to return to the Klamath Reserva-tion, or, for those born in captivity, to go there for the first time.

If one goes by "the number of Indians involved," Keith Murray has observed, "this was the most expensive Indian war the United States ever fought."[22] In these matters, "expensive" carries a host of meanings.

Pattern 11:
Exultation and a sense of achieved glory were hard emotions for the victors to feel at the end of a war; the Indians, at the time of the surrender, looked more like a pitiable and battered people than a fierce and terrifying enemy, valiantly defeated.

When the survivors of war decided to give up, they were likely to be hungry, tattered, demoralized, and, often enough, injured and wounded. Seeing them in this condition, some officials, officers, soldiers, and civilians responded to the end of the war with fits of regret and wishful hindsight, wondering, "Was all this really necessary?" The same outcome could have been reached, many participants would end up thinking, with much less in the way of expense and suffering, using negotiations rather than bullets.

The moment of surrender creates an unsettling dilemma, as well, for historians. Brought together in Helen Hunt Jackson's *Century of Dishonor* (1881) and welded into place by Dee Brown's *Bury My Heart at Wounded Knee* (1971), the standard, sympathetic version of Indian/white history casts Indians as victims, passive people who stood frozen in place as a great wave of white expansion crashed down upon them and left them broken and shattered. This story, of course, was of a piece with a broader approach to the history of people of color, an approach which accented the actions of whites towards the "others," and virtually ignored anything that these "others" did for themselves and on their own terms. In the last twenty years, the rejection of this model of passivity and victimization has become an article of faith among most American historians. Indians—and African Americans and Mexican Americans and Asian Americans—were not passive victims, we all recognize now; they were active participants in making and shaping their own history. We did Indian people a disservice when we adopted what one might call "the hanky at the eye" school of Indian history, thinking of Indians as melancholy victims, boohooing over the injuries of the past, lamenting the Indian "plight," and seeing the whole story as very, very sad.

And yet, at the end of an Indian/white war, reduced by the hardships of life in chronic battle, sometimes betrayed by other Indians, often forcibly removed from the place they considered home, bullied into giving up ownership of that home, the Indians often *did* look like victims, and the whole story does indeed seem very, very sad. It would be silly to ride the pendulum-swing back to the version of history in which the Indians were victims, and nothing but victims. As many of these "Twelve Points of War" suggest, these stories would not make an ounce of sense if one did not see Indians themselves as active forces in the shaping of history. But one ends up shaken in one's orthodoxy. Consider the condition of Indian people at the end of the wars, and the term "victim" keeps coming back to mind. Reciting a declaration of faith—"we just don't think of Indians as victims anymore"—will not drive the word out.

Modoc Story, Part 12

On November 29, 1872, Mrs. Boddy and Mrs. Schira were suddenly and bitterly widowed when Hooker Jim's group killed their husbands. In June of 1873, while the Modocs were held as prisoners of war at Fort Klamath, Colonel Jefferson Davis, the commanding officer at the fort, responded to an alarm. Mrs. Boddy and Mrs. Schira had entered the prisoners' compound. "Mrs. Schira had a double-edged knife in her hand which she was trying to use on Hooker Jim. Mrs. Boddy had a gun which she did not know how to cock."[23] Colonel Davis restrained them and took their weapons.

The depth of bitterness—Modoc to white and white to Modoc—seemed beyond any healing. And yet the American public's fascination with the West and with Indians offered an odd alternative to vengeance. Indians associated with wars of resistance were instant celebrities. Both the Nez Perce Chief Joseph and the Hunkpapa Sitting Bull had barely surrendered before they were being hosted and lionized, interviewed and celebrated, by white Americans. If Captain Jack had *not* taken part in the murder of commissioners during a truce, one suspects that instead of being hanged in October of 1873, he might well have been on a tour of the East Coast, watched by crowds in New York and hosted at a presidential reception in Washington, D.C.

Trying to capitalize on the commercial opportunity presented by the wars, the former superintendent of Indian affairs for Oregon and former peace commissioner Albert Meacham made the most of his injuries. When the Modocs killed Commissioner Eleazar Thomas and General E. R. S. Canby, Commissioner Meacham had been left for dead. Recovered from his many wounds, Meacham went on a prolonged lecture tour, displaying the wounds he received from the Modocs and sometimes displaying the Modocs themselves. Shacknasty Jim, Steamboat Frank, and Scarfaced Charley joined Meacham on his tours. The war turned colorful, quaint, and marketable in an amazingly short time.

Pattern 12:
These wars were often so bitter and so brutal that it is hard to imagine either (a) how the Indian wars ever turned romantic, picturesque, or fun in the hands of American myth-makers, or (b) how the survivors and their descendants were ever able to live in peace with each other.

In the hands of novelists and filmmakers, the Indian/white wars became spectacles with great entertainment value. Here is one of the greatest mysteries of the commercial manipulation of the story of westward expansion: historical episodes in which human nature appeared at its worst provided novelists and movie-makers with the material for escapist fantasies. Escapist? In their true character, these stories raise profound questions about the reality of evil in human life, questions made even more compelling when they arise in a nation which has struggled to paint its history in shades of innocence. Rather than permitting the reader to escape the sorrows and troubles of the real world, these events force the reader's attention to the grimmest facts about American origins. They are moral and spiritual muddles, in which the lines between good guy and bad guy, victim and villain twist and meander and intertwine. And yet by the powerful alchemy of selective story-telling, in American popular culture, narratives of great complexity became simple stories of adventure and heroism and triumph, with, perhaps, just a tinge of melancholy.

Just as mysterious is the process by which peace was restored and a kind of coexistence arranged. When you have at the center of your consciousness a knowledge of the injuries and outrages committed in the course of these wars, a century does not seem like enough time to restore the peace.

A story that westerners tell to make fun of easterners brings this issue to a focus. A car full of tourists from New Jersey pulls up at a gas station in a remote western setting. "We notice there's an Indian reservation up ahead," the tourists say to the gas station attendant. "It's getting close to sunset; are we going to be safe if we try to cross the reservation after dark?"

"Well," says the gas station attendant, whose sister owns the motel next door, "I'd be very careful about that. But your timing is good; the weekly army convoy leaves tomorrow at seven in the morning. If you wanted to get a room at the motel tonight, then you could be sure you'll be safe tomorrow."

This story usually presents a fine opportunity to laugh at the fools of the eastern United States. But when you have been reading the stories of Indian/white warfare, considering the full measure of bitterness and brutality in those events and recognizing how short a period of time a century is, the notion of waiting for the 7 A.M. convoy does not seem like such a foolish idea.

And yet, at some point, the participants in these wars and their descendants broke the cycle of revenge and retaliation, and ceased to think of each other's destruction as a desirable goal. In the United States of the late twentieth century, the descendants of the Modocs and the descendants of the white settlers of northern California and southern Oregon are not killing each other. We take that turn of events for granted, but for someone immersed in the history of the Indian/white wars, this outcome appears remarkable, surprising, and even illogical. Continued theft and manipulation of Indian resources, restrictions on Indian religious freedom, arbitrary and damaging federal intervention in reservation affairs,

poverty, unemployment, alcoholism, discrimination, prejudice, and bitter memories: there is nothing cheering in those various manifestations of the legacy of conquest. But it is still a considerable relief when the flow of blood slows down, and the guns, by and large, fall silent.

AFTER THE WARS:
THE CHARACTER OF AMERICAN SUNLIGHT

In America, the Indian is relegated to the obligatory first chapter—the "Once Great Nation" chapter—after which the Indian is cleared away as easily as brush, using a very sharp rhetorical tool called an "alas."

Richard Rodriguez,
Days of Obligation

Immerse yourself in the history of Indian/white wars, and you gain one advantage that others around you will not have. Along with your neighbors and associates, you may well be disheartened by the alarming violence of the late twentieth century, by the urban gangs, the drug warfare, and the drive-by shootings that leave many feeling precarious and vulnerable. But while others imagine a happier age in the past, when times were less brutal and better values prevailed, the person who has been thinking about the Indian/white wars will waste no time in yearning for a prettier time in the past when humans treated each other better. If you have been reading descriptions of the careful, detailed, exquisite, and very personal torture and mutilation that characterized Indian/white encounters on a number of occasions in the eighteenth and nineteenth centuries, then drive-by shootings acquire a different shading. They are terrible things, but they are not any more terrible than the killings of the Indian/white wars. By some measures, if you compare a nineteenth-century death by torture and mutilation to a twentieth-century death by a comparatively quick and impersonal shooting, the terribleness of violence may seem to be shrinking over time.

Readers may well find themselves rendered unhappy and unsettled by this line of reflection, and especially that curious word, "measures." What, in heaven's name, are the proper "measures" for judging and comparing levels of horror and terror? Numbers are, for many people in the late twentieth century, the standard way of measuring everything: economic well-being, social values, educational achievement, the effectiveness of leaders, success or failure, progress or decline. But should numbers set the level of our response to brutality? Should there be some sort of direct correlation in which the numbers of dead and injured provide a precise setting for our horror and outrage?

Nearly everyone who writes about battles and massacres wrestles, at least briefly, with the problem of numbers. This episode of numerical reflection usually begins with the problem of disputed numbers: battles and massacres are occasions of passion, and passion works against precision in numerical records. It is thus a standard exercise in Battle and Massacre Studies, this deliberation over how many were killed, how many were injured, and how many in both of those categories were women and children.

In the more reflective writers, there is a moment when this quantitative exercise strikes them as odd and troubling. Historian Juanita Brooks, writing about Utah's Mountain Meadows Massacre, offers what may well be the only clearheaded conclusion: "The total number [killed at Mountain Meadows] remains uncertain. We can be sure only that, however many there were, it was too many."[24]

While it certainly made a difference to the individuals involved, should it really make a difference to our judgment of an event—if the total number of casualties at a given massacre added up to 214 or to 198? By the measure of numbers, the comparison between violence in the nineteenth century and violence in the twentieth century clearly works to the disadvantage of our times. In the wars of the twentieth century and the Holocaust in Nazi Germany, the numerical indices of brutality soared off the charts. If you went by the numbers, the violence of the Indian/white wars would hardly register when you put the totals of their casualties up against the millions in the twentieth century. Whatever else we learn from numbers, we learn that twentieth-century human beings do not have much in the way of moral high ground. With its record of wars and holocausts and threatened atomic annihilation, the twentieth century provides no viewers' grandstand on which we can sit in self-righteous judgment of the cruelties of the nineteenth century. Thus, when the writers of a recent American history textbook tell us that "by twentieth century standards, [Andrew] Jackson's Indian policy was both callous and brutal," one cannot help wondering, "And which twentieth century standards are those?"[25]

There is, in any case, not much in the way of opportunity or originality left for late arrivals in the business of moral condemnation. By the 1970s, the federal government, the United States Army, the volunteer regiments, and the resource-grabbing settlers had taken just about every blow that printed words can inflict. The Modoc War, wrote historian Keith Murray in 1959, was "a perfect case study in American maladministration of its Indian affairs." This was "a government that did not know where it was going or what it was doing." The "most serious aspect" of the war, Murray concluded, was that "the federal government clearly learned nothing."[26] In a later history of the war, published in 1973, Richard Dillon was even more outspoken in his criticisms. The "land-lust of white settlers" gave the Modoc War its context, while the "immediate causes were the usual combination of civilian duplicity and pressure on government, a worthless treaty, Indian Bureau bungling (more stupidity than perfidy) and Army folly and overconfidence."[27]

Reading two-decades-old, no-punches-pulled condemnations of the white/Indian wars, one feels a bit like the nineteenth-century prospectors who arrived late for a gold rush. Very much like a hopeful miner arriving at a placer site months after the first discoveries, one finds that earlier arrivals have already taken all the good lines. As much as the latter-day critic might like to land an original blow, the duplicitous federal government and the greedy white settlers have already been beaten around the post, and there is not much left for late arrivals to do, besides regret their timing.

The book reviews that responded to the publication of *Bury My Heart at Wounded Knee* in 1971 provide remarkable evidence of how completely condemnation of the wars had become a litany, a formula, a chant. The periodical *Book World* characterized *Bury My Heart* in these terms:

> Custer may have died for our sins, but Indians still have much to reproach the White Man for. A chronicle of lies, torture, and slaughter on the plains that exhausts anger, pity, and regret. Never again.[28]

Recommending Dee Brown's book as one of the "best books for young adults" for the year, *The Booklist* summed up its content:

> Battle by battle, massacre by massacre, broken treaty by broken treaty, this is a documented, gripping chronicle of the Indian struggle from 1860 to 1890 against the white man's systematic plunder.[29]

To a writer for *Newsweek*, the "appalling" story that Brown told, "with plenty of massacres and genocide overlooked by our traditional history texts," was "essential history for Americans, who must learn that this sort of thing was quite acceptable to the government in Washington."[30] Writing, as well, in *Newsweek,* Geoffrey Wolfe called *Bury My Heart at Wounded Knee* a "damning case against our national roots in greed, perfidy, ignorance and malice."[31] For Peter Farb, in *The New York Review of Books,* Brown's "account of one horror after another endured by the reds at the hands of whites" showed the Indian wars "to be the dirty murders they were."[32] The book reads like "a crime file," *Life Magazine* said, telling the story of the "thirty-year slaughter of Indians; the broken treaties that stole Indian hunting grounds; the inhumane treatment on reservations; . . . the systematic blood lettings, including the massacres of Sand Creek and Wounded Knee—Mylais of a century ago."[33]

These writers, it is clear, had Vietnam on their mind. But America got out of Vietnam and the recitation of wickedness hardly paused. Even when you turn to the kind of historical writing in which blandness and inoffensiveness have been the most prized of virtues, the condemnation of white behavior in the Indian/white wars proves to be severe and unforgiving. Examine these quotations from recent college-level American history textbooks:

Grasping white men were guilty of many additional provocations. They flagrantly disregarded treaty promises, openly seized the land of the Indians, slaughtered their game, and occasionally debauched their women. . . . On several notorious occasions, innocent Indians were killed for outrages committed by their fellow tribesmen; sometimes they were shot just for "sport."[34]

The Western tribes were also victimized by the incompetence and duplicity of those white officials charged with protecting them. . . . The history of relations between the United States and the Native Americans was, therefore, one of nearly endless broken promises. . . . As usual, it was the whites who committed the most flagrant and vicious atrocities.[35]

The whites took away the tribes' sustenance, decimated their ranks, and shoved the remnants into remote and barren corners of their former domain. . . . No historical equation could have been more precise and implacable: The progress of the white settlers meant the death of the Indians. . . . The Indians had no chance against the overwhelming strength of the soldiers and the relentless white settlement of the land.[36]

The government showed little interest in honoring agreements with Indians. . . . [The attack at Sand Creek] was no worse than many incidents in earlier conflicts with Indians and not very different from what was later to occur in guerrilla wars involving American troops in the Philippines and more recently Vietnam.[37]

The whites cloaked their actions with high sounding expressions like "civilization against savagery" and "Manifest Destiny." But the facts were simple: The whites came and took the Indians' land. . . . American policy towards the Indians was a calamity.[38]

Just a brief tour through these simple declarations from both book reviewers and textbook writers produces strange and unexpected results. "Now just a minute here," one surprises oneself by thinking. "Let's not get carried away; it's really quite a bit more complicated than that."

The biggest puzzle in these summations is, of course, their astonishing assumption of simplicity. The stories of the wars are narratives so tangled and dense that they defy clear telling. In these summations, every ounce of that complexity disappears. The diversity of white people and their responses to war are gone. Instead, a coherent, linear, and, most improbable of all, "systematic" process of eliminating Indians takes the place of the actual jumble of motives and intentions, communications and miscommunications, actions and reactions.

The most distressing element of these set pieces of condemnation is the finality of their plots. Nearly every textbook crashes hard into the massacre at Wounded Knee in 1890; the bodies of the Lakota people left in the snow stand for the end of the Indians as significant and distinctive figures in American history. One textbook gives the section, on the Indians in the late nineteenth century, the title "The End of Tribal Life." From this book, students learn that, in the late nineteenth century, the Indians "lost

their special distinctiveness as a culture."[39] "In the end, blacks were oppressed," summarily declares one textbook published in 1989; while "Native Americans were exterminated."[40] In offering this picture of a strange and dreadful finality, the textbook writers no doubt think that they are showing great sympathy for Indians. They are also, of course, killing them off with a thoroughness that the United States Army did not, thank heavens, match. This, surely, is what writer Richard Rodriguez had in mind when he referred to the habit of getting rid of the Indians with "a very sharp rhetorical tool called an 'alas.'"

Read some of these textbooks, and you want to shout, "Hold the presses! These obituaries are premature!" But more surprising, even the best-credentialed, "Sixties Generation," consistent, white-liberal historian responds to the textbook litanies with an urge to defend the army. Take this summation from a western American textbook published in 1984:

The army was at the center of a vicious spiral of hatred, one level of fury escalating into a tier of bloodletting. The highest levels of command of the army should have been held accountable for not protecting Indians against white settlers. Though lesser officers and enlisted men often sympathized with the native, there is not one significant example of the army protecting the Indian under the law.[41]

"Not one significant example"? But it was a common pattern, after a war, for white civilians to want to kill Indians who had surrendered, and for the army to refuse to give them that opportunity. The characterization of the wicked army does not begin to acknowledge the many occasions on which the soldiers ended up in the middle, trying to resist the settlers' demands for unrestrained violence while still trying to control the Indians. The army, of course, did terrible things, but the greater truth about the army was that it was inconsistent—equally inconsistent in both honor and dishonor.

While the peaks of moral condemnation had already been climbed, claimed, and occupied by the early 1970s, no one had made much of a start on the project of fitting the wars into a broader understanding of American history. On the contrary, some of the writers most committed to lamentation over the injuries done to the Indians were also the most effective at declaring the topic closed and finished. With the massacre at Wounded Knee, authors have drawn the curtain on the whole sad story of the conquest—drawn the curtain, driven the audience out of the theatre, locked the doors, and put up a "CLOSED; WILL NOT REOPEN" sign. With the year 1890 standing, not only for the end of the Indian wars, but virtually for the end of the Indians, the whole subject is isolated, stripped of relevance, and denied any consequence for the present.

With Indian/white wars quarantined from significance, American history looks a great deal more appealing. Consider the portrait of westward expansion offered in 1993 by an American historian, called a "national treasure" by his interviewer. Here is Daniel Boorstin's declaration of faith in an inspiring and uplifting version of American history, resting on a cheerful rendering of westward expansion. In the midst of the divided and violent world of the 1990s, Boorstin said,

> community—an emphasis on what brings us together—is what I think is called for in our time. It's what built the American West: People coming by wagon trains, where they made their own systems of law and cooperated in going up and down the mountains and across the prairies to build new towns.[42]

To ask, "What's missing from this picture?" is to belabor the obvious. The tougher question by far is to ask how such a picture of history could carry any credibility at all. Knowledge of the brutality of the Indian wars has been widely distributed for centuries. And yet Daniel Boorstin carries considerable weight and influence when he places the opportunities and achievements of white people at the center of American history, and pushes the conquest of Indians to the margins of the picture.

On behalf of those who join Boorstin in straining for a prettier picture of the nation's past, one has to say this: it is hard to find a way to tell the national story that does justice both to those who benefitted from conquest and those who literally lost ground. It is damned hard to fit the pieces of this puzzle together.

Consider what might seem to be the most remote

subject from the history of the Indian/white wars: the history of white pioneer women. Men, conventional thinking goes, fight the wars; on this topic, of all topics, it ought to be permissible to concentrate on men's history to the exclusion of women. And vice versa: one ought to be able to write the history of white pioneer women with, at the most, a few brief references to the unpleasantness of the Indian/white wars.

Indeed, separation and segregation have been the pattern in the writing of both the histories of Indian wars and of white pioneer women. Here, one can see the fragmentation of the history of the conquest of North America at its peak. That split appears most clearly and concretely in the writings of Dee Brown. Best known for *Bury My Heart at Wounded Knee,* Brown was also the author of another widely read book on the American West: *The Gentle Tamers: Women of the Old Wild West,* a set of portraits of pioneer women. Neither the word "Indian" nor the word "war" appears in the index of *Gentle Tamers.* In the chapter on "The Army Girls," the focus is on the hardships and travels of army wives. There is no attention to the larger process of conquest which brought them those experiences, and no attention to the impact that the "Army Girls'" husbands had on Indian people.[43]

In Brown's strangely unconnected publications, we have the clearest and starkest example of a common pattern. The history of westward expansion has ended up divided into two, utterly separate stories: the sad and disheartening story of what whites did to the Indians; and the colorful and romantic story of what whites did for themselves. The very same writer can, on different occasions, write both of these stories, with no sense of self-contradiction or inconsistency.

These stories, however, move back together the moment one gives up the campaign to keep them apart. The history of pioneer women and the history of Indian war, to use the examples that seem the most separate, are very much intertwined. Women may have carried some technical status as noncombatants, but that status gave them no exemption from injury. Both white and Indian families were the targets of direct attack, and the deaths of soldiers and warriors in battle left widowed women on both sides facing very tough times. Women could, as well, be powerful forces in demanding revenge and retaliation. The seizure and rape of Indian women, or the forced captivity of white women, were often primary motivations in going to war. For Indian men, the mistreatment of Indian women could be the last straw in the insults of conquest; for white men, the idea of a white woman vulnerable to an Indian man's sexual desire could produce wild and irrational anger.

These connections between women and war are, however, the easy ideas to grasp. The tougher part is recognizing the connection between the wars and the white women settlers who were not direct participants in combat, but who were nonetheless beneficiaries of the opportunities, resources, and lands opened up by the conquest and displacement of Indians. To call white pioneer women "beneficiaries of conquest" is by no means to say that their lives were easy or privileged; on the contrary, their hardships were often grueling. Moreover, many of the pioneer women, whose diaries and memoirs are now available to us, were likable women, women on whom the labels "cruel conqueror," "thoughtless invader," or "villainous displacer of native people" would sit awkwardly. They seem, truly, to have lived in a world apart from the world of massacre, mutilation, torture, and murder.

But did they?

"Although they do not ignore the reality of racist attitudes among white women," historian Antonia Castaneda has said of recent historians writing about white pioneer women, "their accounts are remarkably free of intercultural conflict in a land bloodied by three centuries of war and conquest." These writers ignore "the economic and other privileges that women of the conquering group derive from the oppression of women and men of the group being conquered." Conquest was not the exclusive enterprise of white men: "Within their gender spheres and based upon the power and privilege of their race and class," Castaneda writes, "Euro-American men and women expanded the geo-political-economic area of the United States" and played their part in establishing the dominance of white Americans.[44]

Even if the vast majority of them never fired a gun on a battlefield, much less took part in mutilation at a massacre, white pioneer women were members of a civilian invading force and beneficiaries of the subordination of the natives. A recognition of the moral complexity of their position in history does these women no disservice; on the contrary, it gives a much deeper meaning to their lives by restoring them to their full, tragic context. Putting the history of white pioneer women back together with the history of Indian war is in truth a matter of uniting American history, not disuniting it.

In recent years, Arthur Schlesinger, Jr., speaking for many other traditional American historians, has used the phrase "Disuniting of America" to characterize efforts to write multicultural history. To Schlesinger and his fellows, taking the history of people of color seriously—too seriously—has splintered American history into fragments. And yet, with a quick shift of perspective, what Schlesinger sees as a route to a disintegrated American history can become, instead, the most direct approach to an integrated story. Removing English-speaking white Americans from center-stage, while revaluing the history of people of color, in fact, serves the cause of the "Uniting of America." When, for instance, you release the history of the Indian/white wars from its quarantine as a sad, but irrelevant chapter of history, you make America whole.

You do not, however, make America happy.

In *The Disuniting of America*, Schlesinger acknowledges the injuries of conquest. "White settlers," Schlesinger writes, with expert brevity, "had systematically pushed the American Indians back, killed their braves [*sic*], seized their lands, and sequestered their tribes." That unpleasant business acknowledged, Schlesinger instantly reasserts the quarantine and returns to a vision of American history that concentrates on Anglo-Americans and the unified and harmonic values of their "American Creed." There is room for people of color in this model, but only when they comply with stern rules of admissions. "The ethnic upsurge," Schlesinger remarks, "has had some healthy consequences. The republic has at last begun to give long-overdue recognition to the role and achievements of groups subordinated and ignored during the high noon of male Anglo-Saxon dominance— women, Americans of South and East European ancestry, black Americans, Indians, Hispanics, and Asians." Here, Schlesinger spells out his admissions requirements for historical significance: "There is far better understanding today of the indispensable contributions minorities have made to American civilization."[45]

"Indispensable contributions," it seems likely, is a phrase that does not include the Indian/white wars. When Schlesinger refers to the "achievements" of minorities, one suspects that he does not mean to include the Ohio Confederacy's solid and unambiguous defeats of the United States Army in the 1780s and the 1790s, the defeat of the United States Army by the Modocs on the foggy day of January 17, 1873, or the elimination of Lt. Colonel George Armstrong Custer and his men at Little Big Horn in 1876. The phrase "indispensable contributions" probably does not refer to the desperate struggle of the Sauk and Fox people to cross the Mississippi at the mouth of the Bad Axe River before the firearms of soldiers and the guns of a warship could strike them down, nor to the Shoshone blood that stained the snow at Bear River in southern Idaho in 1863, nor to the futile efforts of Black Kettle and White Antelope at Sand Creek to tell John Chivington's men that their people were at peace and not at war.

The battles and the massacres cannot slip smoothly into a model of a benevolent white majority helped out by positively participating minorities. The battles and the massacres blow apart any attempt to construct a "happy-face" version of American history, in which minorities make "indispensable contributions" and everyone has a nice day. But if these stories dismantle an artificial form of national unity, they provide the basis for another, much more convincing and grounded kind of integration, for another kind of historical wholeness.

Cease to quarantine the Indian/white wars, battles, and massacres, and you take an essential step toward the uniting of American history. Nineteenth-century white pioneer women and twentieth-century white career women, exploiters of natural resources and celebrators of natural beauty, rural cowboys and urban businessmen, bluebloods of Boston whose ancestors arrived in the 1620s and Mexican immigrants who arrived yesterday: a whole range of people who see each other as alien and who feel that they have no common ground, benefit from the tragic events of conquest. Conquest wove a web of consequences that does indeed unite the nation. We are all in this together.

We live, every one of Drex Brooks's photographs tells us, on haunted land, on land that is layers deep in human passion and memory. There is, today, no longer any point in sorting out these passions and memories into starkly separate forms of ownership. Whether or not the majority who died at any particular site were Indians or whites, these places literally ground Americans of all backgrounds in their common history. In truth, the tragedies of the wars are our national joint property, and how we handle that property is the test of our unity or disunity, maturity or immaturity, as a people wearing the label "American."

For a century or two, white American intellectuals labored under the notion that the United States was sadly disadvantaged when it came to the joint property of history. The novelist Henry James gave this conviction of American cultural inferiority its most memorable statement. Writing of Nathaniel Hawthorne, James explained that Hawthorne was a novelist working against the odds. As an American, he was stuck trying to craft deep literature from the thin material of American history. The richness of European history was simply not to be found in Massachusetts. The "flower of art blooms only where the soil is deep," James said; "it takes a great deal of history to produce a little literature." And then James offered one of the most memorable of dismissals and brush-offs:

> History, as yet, has left in the United States but so thin and impalpable a deposit that we very soon touch the hard substratum of nature, and nature herself in the western world, has the peculiarity of seeming rather crude and immature. The very air looks new and young; the light of the sun seems fresh and innocent, as if it knew as yet but few of the secrets of the world and none of the weariness of shining;. . . . A large juvenality is stamped upon the face of things, and in the vividness of the present, the past, which died so young and had time to produce so little, attracts but scanty attention.[46]

"The past, which died so young and had time to produce so little": twenty years ago, when I first read it, this remark put me into a frenzy. My first impulse was to resurrect Henry James and pack him off to Mesa Verde, or to any number of other sites of long-term human occupation in the "New" World. But my second impulse, shaped by my reckoning with Drex Brooks's project in photography, is to spare James the hardship of either temporal or geographical travel. My wish now is really quite workable: simply to ask everyone who is tempted to share in James's lament to pause for a moment to think about the Indian/white wars.

Place the stories of the wars next to James's image of a nation without deep or consequential history, and you at once dissolve and solve the problem of historical thinness that so worried James and others like him. The wars work equally as well as correctives for the concerns of contemporary historians like Daniel Boorstin and Arthur Schlesinger, Jr., struggling to write American history in positive and uplifting terms, under the conviction that an upbeat telling of history works for the nation's benefit. And yet the inadvertent side effect of their campaign for historical cheer is to return us to the condition that Henry James lamented—to cast the United States, once again, as the exceptional part of the planet, the place where the "light of the sun seems fresh and innocent, as if it knew as yet but few of the secrets of the world and none of the weariness of shining."

Shining on North America, the sun that now lights Brooks's photographs long ago gave up its claim on innocence. Illuminating the events of the Indian/white wars, the sun came to know quite a few of the most unsettling "secrets" of human nature. To try to forget those secrets diminishes the human spirit. And that, to the best of my understanding, is the point of Drex Brooks's work.

NOTES

1. Note 115, Donald Jackson, editor, *Black Hawk: An Autobiography* (Urbana: University of Illinois Press, 1964), 138–39.

2. Robert Utley, "Foreword," in Editors of Time-Life Books, *The Old West* (New York: Prentice-Hall Press, 1990), 7; Gerald D. Nash, *Creating the West: Historical Interpretations, 1890–1990* (Albuquerque: University of New Mexico Press, 1991), 143–44.

3. Patricia Nelson Limerick, *The Legacy of Conquest: The Unbroken Past of the American West* (New York: W. W. Norton, 1987), 349.

4. My telling of this story draws on an unpublished manuscript: Patricia Nelson Limerick, "What's in a Name? Nichols Hall: A Report," 1987. This was a study prepared at the request of James Corbridge, Chancellor of the University of Colorado at Boulder, to evaluate the propriety of retaining the name (applied to a campus building) of a white participant at Sand Creek.

5. John Smith, "The Chivington Massacre," U.S. Senate, *Reports of the Joint Special Committees on the Conditions of the Indian Tribes,* Sen. Report 156, 39th Cong., 2d sess., 1967, 42.

6. Lt. James D. Cannon, U.S. Senate, "Massacre of the Cheyenne Indians," *Report of the Joint Committee on the Conduct of War,* Sen. Report 142, 38th Cong., 2d sess., 1865, 88–89.

7. Dave Louderbeck, "Sand Creek Massacre," *Report of the Secretary of War,* Sen. Exec. Doc. 26, 39th Cong., 2d sess., 1867, 137.

8. For the story of the Modoc War, I have drawn on Keith A. Murray, *The Modocs and Their War* (Norman: University of Oklahoma Press, 1959); Richard Dillon, *Burnt-Out Fires* (Englewood Cliffs, N.J.: Prentice-Hall, 1973); and Francis S. Landrum, compiler, *Guardhouse, Gallows and Graves: The Trial and Execution of Indian Prisoners of the Modoc Indian War by the U.S. Army* (Klamath Falls, Ore.: Klamath County Museum, 1988).

9. Dillon, *Burnt-Out Fires,* 157.

10. Murray, *Modocs and Their War*, 105.

11. Dillon, *Burnt-Out Fires*, 158.

12. "Proceedings of a Military Commission Convened at Fort Klamath, Oregon, for the Trial of Modoc Prisoners," Appendix B, in Landrum, *Guardhouse, Gallows, and Graves*, 126 and 128.

13. Murray, *Modocs and Their War*, 125 and 238.

14. Ibid., 231 and 236.

15. Ibid., 237, 241.

16. Dillon, *Burnt-Out Fires*, 260.

17. Murray, *Modocs and Their War*, 277.

18. Dillon, *Burnt-Out Fires*, 178.

19. Mae T. Parry, "Massacre at Boa Ogoi," Appendix B, in Brigham D. Madsen, *The Shoshoni Frontier and the Bear River Massacre* (Salt Lake City: University of Utah Press, 1985), 235.

20. "Proceedings," Landrum, *Guardhouse, Gallows, and Graves*, 86, 95, and 125.

21. Murray, *Modocs and Their War*, 301.

22. Ibid., 309.

23. Ibid., 274.

24. Juanita Brooks, *The Mountain Meadows Massacre* (Norman: University of Oklahoma Press, 1964), xviii.

25. James Kirby Martin, Randy Roberts, Steven Mintz, Linda O. McMurry, and James H. Jones, *America and Its People* (Glenview, Ill.: Scott, Foresman, 1989), 282.

26. Murray, *Modocs and the War*, 313–16.

27. Dillon, *Burnt-Out Fires*, vii.

28. *Bookworld* (vol. 5), December 5, 1971.

29. *The Booklist* (vol. 68), April 1972, 663–64.

30. *Newsweek* (vol. 78), December 27, 1971, 57.

31. *Newsweek* (vol. 77), February 1, 1971, 69.

32. Peter Farb, "Indian Corn," *New York Review of Books* (vol. 17), December 16, 1971, 36–38.

33. *Life* (Vol. 70), April 2, 1971, 9.

34. Thomas A. Bailey and David M. Kennedy, *The American Pageant: a History of the Republic*, 9th ed. (Lexington, Mass.: Heath, 1991), 588.

35. Alan Brinkley, Richard N. Current, Frank Freidel, and T. Harry Williams, *American History: A Survey*, 8th ed. (New York: McGraw-Hill, 1991), 501 and 504.

36. James A. Henretta, W. Elliott Brownlee, David Brody, and Susan Ware, *America's History* (Chicago: Dorsey, 1987), 597.

37. John A. Garraty, *The American Nation: A History of the United States*, 7th ed. (New York: HarperCollins, 1991), 489.

38. R. Jackson Wilson, James Gilbert, Stephen Nissenbaum, Karen Ordahl Kupperman, and Donald Scott, *The Pursuit of Liberty: A History of the American People*, 2d ed. (Belmont, Calif.: Wadsworth, 1990), 682 and 688.

39. Divine, pp. 502–4.

40. Martin, et al., *America and Its People*, 503.

41. Robert Hine, *The American West: A Interpretive History*, 2d ed. (Boston: Little, Brown, 1984), 212.

42. Tad Szulc, "The Greatest Danger We Face," *Parade*, July 25, 1993, 4–7.

43. Dee Brown, *Bury My Heart at Wounded Knee: An Indian History of the American West* (New York: Holt, Rinehart & Winston, 1971) and *The Gentle Tamers: Women of the Old Wild West* (1958; Lincoln: University of Nebraska Press, 1968).

44. Antonia I. Castaneda, "Women of Color and the Rewriting of Western History: The Discourse, Politics,

and Decolonization of History," *Pacific Historical Review* 61, no. 4 (November 1992):520–21.

45. Arthur M. Schlesinger, Jr., *The Disuniting of America: Reflections on a Multicultural Society* (New York: Whittle Direct Books, 1991), 14 and 2.

46. Henry James, *Hawthorne* (rpt. 1887; New York: AMS Press, 1968), 3, 12, 13.